My Kids Are All Grown Up, So Why Are They Still Driving Me Crazy?

How To Get Along With Your Adult Children, Their Spouses and Other Aliens

Bea Lewis
with
MARILYN MURRAY WILLISON

Copyright © 2011 Bea Lewis with Marilyn Murray Willison
All rights reserved.

ISBN: 1460954904
ISBN-13: 9781460954904

Library of Congress Control Number: 2011905683

DEDICATION

To my daughters – Laurie, Jennifer and Kimberly – the most precious jewels on earth. Thank you for teaching me compassion, forgiveness and understanding, and for giving your dad and me six magnificent grandchildren. And to my husband, Ed, for sharing my journey through life and keeping me sane.

B. L.

To my sons – B.G. and Geoffrey – who have taught me how rewarding motherhood can be; to Tori and Susan for being ideal daughters-in-law; and to Cara, Morgan, Ivy and Gray, who are my next generation of teachers. And, of course, Tony, who makes everything possible.

M.M.W.

TABLE OF CONTENTS

Chapter   **Page**

Introduction 1

1. You May Be Big, But You're Still My Kid:
Keeping them close but letting them go. . . . 9

2. A Cain and Abel Rerun:
Understanding the dynamics of adult sibling rivalry 23

3. Money Matters – To Aid or Not To Aid:
Learning the difference between helping and enabling. 39

4. Gay, But Not Happy:
Accepting gay and lesbian children 55

5. The Boomerang Kid:
When Big Bird returns to the nest. 69

6. The Rabbi, The Priest, and Thou:
Dealing with a child's interfaith marriage. . 85

7. **Mirror, Mirror On The Wall,
   Who's The Favorite Grandma of All?**
   Competition between sets of grandparents . 97

8. **Women at War: Making Friends With Your
   Daughter-in-Law:**
   The underlying conflicts of loving the
   same man 111

9. **Divorce American Style:**
   Adapting to new family dynamics, especially
   when there are grandchildren 129

10. **My Mother, My Self:**
    Seeing your daughter as she wants
    to be seen 149

INTRODUCTION

"The challenge of parenting adult children is a lot like feeding alligators. If you stay too far way, the alligators could starve – if you get too close, you might get your head bitten off."

Unknown

The kids are grown and your parenting job is done. Now go out and enjoy your life. Right? Dream on.

Who are those people who: live together before marriage; live miles apart from us; delay marriage; divorce at whim; avoid commitment; don't want to hear a thing we have to say or think nothing of spending what they don't have? Who are these people who raise our grandchildren on fast food and mega doses of medication to keep them calm and take the same pills themselves to stay tranquil? They are our adult children, and they are living in a rapidly-changing, fast-paced society that causes us to scratch our heads in wonderment. It's important for us to remember that as the world changes, so does our relationship with our grown children.

The idea for this guide was born during a conversation I had with a group of friends who were relaxing poolside in our South Florida over-55 community. As we smeared on the sunscreen, my group of a dozen or so ladies talked about everything from the trips we've taken, the best plastics surgeons in the area, and which early-bird specials were worth eating before five PM. And more often than not, we'd swap stories about our adult children.

Outwardly, the talks about our kids were laced with humor, but inwardly we all seemed to be grappling with ways to have a better relationship with them now that they were grown. Collectively, we had a myriad of concerns and disappointments. One friend's daughter had adopted a child with her lesbian partner. While excited to become a first-time grandmother, my neighbor feared negative responses from her friends and relatives. Another friend was devastated about her son's recent divorce, and saddened that she could only see her grandchildren on *daddy's* weekend. While one mother's turmoil revolved around her daughter's constant request for money, another expressed her loneliness; her kids hardly ever called.

I was happy to listen to their issues and concerns, and more than willing to share my own parenting experiences with them in return. What I didn't tell my friends was that the reason I was able to withhold passing judgment or avoid being critical was because years ago I had learned that "what's not your problem today, just might be your burden tomorrow." And before I knew it, I'd established a website to serve as an online home for addressing those types of problems (www.bealewis.com).

Because of my journalism background, (as a retired staff writer for the prestigious New York newspaper, **Newsday**) I proposed an idea for an advice column about "parent/adult child relationships" to the **Palm Beach Post** newspaper when we relocated to Florida. The editors loved it, and for five years I offered readers – on a weekly basis – suggestions and advice from a variety of experts, including Dr. Holly

Katz, brilliant Clinical Director of the Group Counseling Center in Boca Raton, Florida. And much of what I learned from her and other family-relationship experts is shared on the following pages.

If you are struggling to understand your children who are in their 20's, 30's, 40's and older – and make sense of how they live today – this guide is for you. You will learn how to step back and let your adult children make their own decisions without feeling you failed them, or how to respect them as individuals who have different views of how to live their lives. You may not be able to change a situation in your child's life that you don't like, but in this book you will learn how to change your *perception* of your child's state of affairs that upsets you. And in the process you'll learn how to view challenging situations as a positive instead of a negative.

Because we are living longer, we will be in the parenting business with our adult kids for many more years than we were when our children were little. This guide is designed to help you during the "second stage" parenting phase – by outlining specific ways to deal with the issues new to our generation.

The following chapters will help you:

- Learn new adult-to-adult communication skills. Suggestions from the experts will help you to learn how to effectively express your thoughts and feelings as well as know when to give advice or when to just sit back and listen. (Chapter One)
- Acquire skills to help you sidestep your adult children's sibling rivalry. (Chapter Two)
- Recognize if you have become your child's personal ATM machine, and realize the difference between **helping** and enabling your child. (Chapter Three)
- Learn how – if you're having trouble acknowledging that your son or daughter is gay – to come to terms with that reality. It will help everyone involved if you can love and accept your whole child, rather than be conflicted over his or her sexual orientation. (Chapter Four)
- Get along with your grown kids who return to the nest after college or who come back to the cocoon due to a job loss or the end of a

marriage. This chapter will include proactive tips for real-life issues like keeping a) peace in a multigenerational house, b) adequate amounts of food in the refrigerator, and c) utility bill charges from going into overload. (Chapter Five)
- Accept your child's interfaith marriages and resist imposing your viewpoints when the grandchildren are being raised in a faith so foreign from that in which you raised their parents. (Chapter Six)
- Learn to accept competition with the other set of grandparents. (Chapter Seven)
- Find ways to communicate better with your daughter-in-law, so that she becomes a friend rather than competition. (Chapter Eight)
- Understand what to do when your children divorce and how to effectively cope with your anguish when the grandchildren are shuffled between mommy and daddy's households (family relationships were much simpler in our day when most folks stayed

married and children lived under one roof). (Chapter Nine)
- Discover what to say to a daughter to help her understand that you don't want to run her life, but that you do care. (Chapter Ten)

This book can't give you a solution for all the potential problems you may have with your adult children. For example, if your family is struggling with an adult child who is enmeshed in chronic destructive behavior, then everyone involved needs to seek professional advice and support. But this book does contain a wealth of effective suggestions to help you learn specific tools designed to ease the transition from parenting your children when they were young, to maintaining a fulfilling and positive relationship with them as adults.

CHAPTER ONE

YOU MAY BE BIG, BUT YOU'RE STILL MY KID
Keeping them close but letting them go

"Our children are not going to be 'our children' forever; they are going to be other people's wives, husbands, and the parents of our grandchildren."

Dr. Mary S. Calderone

Are you a helicopter mom or dad who hovers over your children even though they are grown? Or are you the sort of parent who is willing to let go of the controls and enjoy a more pleasurable, satisfying and adult-to-adult relationship?

I learned my first lesson about letting go of my role as Mother Hen to my grown children when Lyn – my first granddaughter – was a baby. They lived in Baltimore; I was in New York. It was Lyn's first illness, she had the flu, and was running a fever that spiked at 104 degrees. Since I lived hundreds of miles away, I worried that her young parents wouldn't be able to care for her the way I would if I lived close by. So I would call constantly.

I was one of those unintentionally annoying helicopter moms, who was hovering over my children, and doing so at a stressful time. If the young parents weren't already nervous enough, I was making them totally crazy with my neurotic fears and out-of-date advice. (We now know that alcohol baths are dangerous for babies!) Although they were grown adults and living on their own, I still couldn't find a comfortable place to land and let go of the controls.

After the tenth call in two days, my son-in-law calmly said, "Please don't call again. I promise that we will call you, and let you know when she gets better."

It was that *aha* moment when I realized that Joe and Jen were the parents-in-charge, and they had drawn an invisible boundary line to let me know what I could – or could not – do regarding their child. That was my first of many lessons on how to let go of *the parent I used to be when my children were little,* and work toward being *the parent I needed to be in the here and now.*

For most of us, the process of letting go is a double-edged sword. On one hand, we encourage our kids' independence, but on the other hand, we want them to stay close and attached. So it's easy to understand that the sentiment "you may be big, but you're still my kid" underlies the main conflict between parents and their adult children. For me, letting go of my role as a mom meant losing my identity as the most important and cherished person in my daughters' lives! They had grown up, and now it was time for me to change, as well.

Here, in a nutshell, is the rub. Adult kids want to be treated as grown ups, but we find it difficult to stop parenting. After all, we dedicated two or more decades to pouring our heart and soul into our precious offspring, as Charlotte did with her son, Bobby. And then, all of a sudden, we're out of a job.

Charlotte's Story

"If I close my eyes, I can scroll back to the days when this sweet little guy would run to me whenever he saw me waiting for him outside his kindergarten class. I was the love of his life; he adored me. After school, our routine was to head for the library, and then to the ice cream store; just the two of us, hand in hand. Those were such happy years!

"Even as a teenager, when most children break away from their parents, Bobby and I remained close. I no longer had to drive him to the library (he had his own car), but we'd spend the dinner hour talking first about his day, and then I'd tell him about mine. Who could ask for a better friend?

"When Bobby when off to college, I lost my pal. He called now and then, but after a while, the phone calls – even the emails – became few and far between. When we did talk, he would get annoyed with my questions about campus life. I felt sad; he had become so distant. I missed my kid, and didn't understand why he was shutting me out."

"It wasn't that Bobby was shutting Charlotte out," explained Dr. Holly Katz, Clinical Director of the Center for Group Counseling in Boca Raton, Florida. "Bobby was doing something completely normal and healthy – he was separating from his mother, a job he'd started when his umbilical cord was cut. And, little by little, he's been trying to make the transition into becoming his own person."

When Charlotte expressed concern, Bobby felt smothered. When she offered advice, he felt she was bossing him. Dr. Katz suggested that she give her son a little space and enough room to make that transition. Charlotte, of course, can keep the lines of communication open, but she should also consider finding a new, more appropriate "pal," a contemporary with whom she can share common interests.

At any stage, letting go, or what child development experts call "the separation process," is not an easy task for either the parent or the child.

> ***TAKE AWAY:*** *Your children are not in your life to serve as your best friend or as your social safety net.*

Most "parents of a certain age" are smart enough to know that our kids are no longer children, yet too often we can't resist telling them what to do. If your kids convey the message that you are overbearing and/or annoying because you are committing the sin of always giving them "**unsolicited advice**," maybe you can relate to Carol's story.

Carol's Story

Carol was disappointed when her son, Jeff, and his wife of ten years, Sara, went house hunting. Initially, she was excited for them and (having owned a number of homes in her lifetime) was looking forward to giving them both the benefit of her experience and advice.

But when the time came for the couple to look around, not only did Sara and Jeff not invite Carol along with them, they avoided her queries about what they'd found. "It was hurtful. They were keeping it all so hush, hush," she said, which made her feel left out and useless.

Dr. Katz explained to me that it wasn't about the young couple "keeping secrets" from Carol. It was about them wanting to savor and control this exciting big step in their young lives that of buying their first home together.

When Jeff and Sara were asked why they didn't include Carol, they explained that they wanted to be free to make their own decision, rather than be influenced by what Carol had to say. "Her opinions," added Sara, "would reflect what she likes, not necessarily what we would want."

When Carol realized why the young couple avoided her advice, she began to understand that this first big purchase should reflect **their** needs. The house selection process was not meant to be about her desire to be needed.

It took time for Carol to get over her hurt, but when Sara and Jeff hosted their first housewarming party, Carol wisely bragged to everyone about how proud she was of the first-time homebuyers.

> ***TAKE AWAY:*** *Good parenting allows adult children to make their own decisions. Parental advice is rarely welcome unless it's asked for.*

It took Joe much longer to give up the controls to his two sons, Bill and Ritchie.

Joe's Story

Joe had always planned for them to take over his successful retail business when he was ready to retire. The boys had worked at their dad's clothing store since their early teens, and now that they had both graduated from college with degrees in Business Administration, Joe felt that it was time to turn the business over to them. But it was a tough transition for him to relinquish control. Even though he was officially "retired", he would call his sons daily to get updates and give them advice based on his many years of experience.

Bill and Ritchie, in contrast, had many new ideas they had learned in graduate school, like using the Internet to sell their clothing line. This was confusing to Joe, and the two generations were soon locked in terrible conflict. "I know this business inside and out. Am I supposed to keep all that knowledge to myself?" Joe grumbled. He grew depressed, and often thought of taking the business back from his sons.

"Transfers of family businesses are often fraught with pitfalls," according to Gary Buffone, the author of ***Choking on the Silver Spoon.*** And for men like Joe, who retired early, it's more of a challenge if the man's identity is invested in his former career or job.

Joe was no longer the "boss" of the business, and telling his children "the way to do things" was his way of hanging on to his former identity. Joe's wife recognized his difficulty and made plans for more of a social life to keep him busy and satisfied. Joe learned to play golf and poker. As his days became busier, he was less concerned about the business and how his sons were running it. The more leeway he gave them, the more confident the sons became, and the business grew to be more successful.

Bill and Ritchie did call their dad from time to time to ask for his advice, and most of the time Joe was happy to give it – but not always. Recently, he didn't even hear their phone call. Why? Joe was underwater snorkeling on vacation in the Caribbean!

> ***TAKE AWAY:*** *The more trust and confidence you show your adult children, the more you empower them to make good decisions.*

While parents are not always aware of it, making your kids feel guilty ("Woe is me: I don't mind sitting in the dark by myself") is a common way many parents **try** to exert control over their adult children. But rest assured, this method (though popular) almost always backfires, just as it did in Rosalind's case.

Rosalind's Story

Rosalind went ballistic when her daughter and son-in-law announced that they were moving across country, from New York (where she lived) to California. "It was like they stuck a knife in my heart," she said. "How could they do this to me? How will I see the grandchildren grow up? What will happen if I become ill? After all, I'm a widow now. And, she added, "what will the neighbors think when they find out that they're leaving their poor mother behind?" Rosalind didn't sleep for nights after hearing the unwelcome news.

She decided to let them know what she had sacrificed for them, how she had given up her whole life for them; Rosalind exaggerated her sense of virtue and devotion at every opportunity. She believed that if she played the guilt card, she could – and would – get her kids to change their mind.

As much as they tried to explain their reasons to Rosalind, she wouldn't listen. It was no wonder that the young family left with barely saying goodbye to her. Rosalind continued to fight for their return, giving them a litany of her aches and pains and loneliness every time she spoke with them. The conversations were full of her complaints rather than her interest in how the grandkids were doing, or how well her son-in-law liked his new job.

After a while, her children didn't even bother to pick up the phone when the caller I.D. identified that it was Rosalind. It's pretty clear that those of us (like Rosalind) who rely on guilt-inducing manipulation simply don't have healthier coping strategies for the times when we feel abandoned or neglected. A social worker at the Senior Center where Rosalind plays Canasta twice a week made a few suggestions that were helpful to her. "Guilt won't make your kids come back to New York, and even if it does, they would act resentful towards you. And that would really not make you feel much better at all," she said.

Instead, the social worker advised Rosalind to focus on broadening her network of friends, including a support system to call on if she got sick and needed some help. Rosalind took the social worker's advice, and joined a group of widowed women who meet twice weekly for lunch and talk. She found them to be helpful when she needed some emotional support, and Rosalind soon learned how to be giving and helpful to them in return.

> ***TAKE AWAY:*** *Secure parents allow their adult children to follow their own dreams.*

CHAPTER WRAP-UP

- Avoid giving unsolicited advice, but be available when asked for it. Resist the feeling of wanting to be needed; it's about their needs, not yours. Before offering advice, ask if they want your opinion.
- The more you tell your children what to do, the less confident they will be to make decisions on their own. Remember that it's okay for grown kids to make mistakes; that's how they learn and become independent. (Didn't we?)

- Acknowledge that you may feel sad, even grieve when your adult child pulls away from you. You're not really being abandoned; it's all just part of the natural process of growing up. Embrace it.
- Recognize that we live in a different world with new rules regarding how it operates. Our advice, no matter how loving the sentiment, can be outdated. The greatest gift you can give your adult child is to express confidence in his or her own decisions.
- Work towards making an independent life of your own; don't make the mistake of relying on your children to create your happiness.

CHAPTER TWO

A CAIN AND ABEL RERUN
Understanding Adult Sibling Rivalry

"My sister is an Only Child."

Steve Solomon, comedian

The other day my husband and I looked through photos from the years when our three daughters were little. "Where did the years go?" I asked Ed as I handed him a photo of the girls (who at the time were six, eight and ten years old) wearing their ice-skating outfits, the pretty ones for the local competitions.

"I remember the day that picture was taken," he blurted out, interrupting the tune of "Sunrise, Sunset," that was playing in my head. "Don't you remember the hysterics that ensued on the ride home because Jen came in first place, but the other two didn't win?" "Oh, yes," I answered. "That was when we thought we had superior parenting skills because we had appeased the two who lost, all the while figuring that the first-place winning eight year old didn't need any additional applause. That was what we assumed, until Jen asked, in a quiet yet determined voice, "Why are you ignoring me? Wasn't I the winner?" GULP!

A similar experience happened when the three girls tried out for the high school cheerleading squad. Only Kim made the team. The jealousy mode in our house went into overdrive. This time we praised Kim with a special dinner; only to have the other two ask why we didn't care about *their* losses. Somehow Ed and I always had trouble getting the "we love you equally" stuff straight.

But now they are grown, are really good friends (most of the time), and are there for each other in times of need (most of the time). That painful, long-ago sibling rivalry is something from the past. Or is it? Sometimes "yes," other times "no."

The worst is when they suspect that Ed and I have spend more time babysitting for one set of grandchildren, but less with another (and, yes, they do keep track of the times). Or when they imagine that a gift given to one daughter is greater in value than what we gave to another (and, yes, they do compare.)

So when did this all start? It begins earlier than you think. According to experts, the problem is basically one of competition for limited resources – a mother's love, approval and time. Frequently, it can start even earlier when a mother brings home a new baby sister or brother, and the older child (or children) becomes keenly aware of having to give up being the sole focus of his or her parents' love.

While humans seem to inherently have sibling rivalry issues ,that's not the case for eagles. For these birds, the solution is easy. According to legend, the mother eagle has her baby eaglets in a nest located somewhere high on a mountainside. The fist eaglet to be born pushes the eggs that contain other future eaglets out of the nest and off the mountain top. Now that the first-born eaglet has insured that he will have mom all to himself, he is guaranteed that there will be no limitations on access to his most important resource – food!

But let's get back to the human species, where what begins as a struggle for mom's attention and approval soon grows into a battle over who gets the bigger dessert, the nicest stuffed animal, or (the very worst) who gets the most valuable Christmas present. Fast forward a few years, and the competition becomes about who has the largest house, the most successful career, or the most money. Sometimes, though, the competition is over silly stuff, like what happened to June.

June's Story

June told me about her two grown sons who one year not only evaluated each other's Christmas gifts, but compared the cards she had attached to the gifts, as well. One son, she said, noticed that his brother's card said "I love you" twice; but she had only written it once on his card! Of course, she said, "I had to defend myself and explain to my son that I'd meant to write the same message on both tags, but the night was late and I was tired." She actually found herself apologizing for her "hurtful" mistake!

> ***TAKE AWAY:** No matter how trivial the object, siblings keep a mental scorecard. Be sensitive to their feelings. Sibling rivalry goes on forever.*

At what age does this sibling jealousy end? I am convinced that it can last an entire lifetime. At one of my speaking engagements, Barbara , who is an 80-something, bleached blonde great-grandmother shared her personal tale of sibling rivalry between her 60 year-old son and her daughter, who was three years younger. (Please note their ages!)

Barbara's Story

Barbara – who lived in Florida – had received an invitation to her son's third wedding, which would take place in Los Angeles. Since she was recuperating from hip surgery, she wasn't strong enough to travel and couldn't attend. A few months later, her daughter – who lived in Chicago – invited Barbara to her 25th wedding anniversary celebration. Feeling better, Barbara agreed to travel to that party.

Soon after, she received an angry phone call from her son, who plaintively asked why she cared enough to attend the sister's party, but not his wedding. It didn't take long for this great grandmother to realize that her son (now a grandfather himself) was jealous, just as he had been in childhood, when he had always made sure that his ice cream serving was the same size as what she had spooned out for his sister!

> **TAKE AWAY:** *Even when they are Senior Citizens, siblings still want to feel that they are number one.*

If the Creator couldn't prevent Cain from killing his brother, Abel, in a jealous rage, why do you think you can singlehandedly minimize your adult kids' jealousies, and downsize the rivalry in their relationships? One multi-layered coping suggestion is to "...accept each child as an individual, and avoid comparisons," said Dr. Michele Borba, author of ***The Big Book of Parenting Solutions.*** That advice would have been helpful to my friend, Brenda, had she known about it earlier.

Brenda's Story

Brenda had confided in me about the angry feelings she had toward one of her daughters who seemed to always ignore her birthday or anniversary: she didn't even bother to send a Mother's Day card. Her two other daughters consistently went out of their way to do special things for her – and always managed to get a sweet card or a little gift sent on time. "I raised all three girls the same way, so how come one daughter can't do the right thing while the other two always do?" she asked. "It isn't really a matter of black and white," I told her. "Just because your daughter doesn't acknowledge the special days that are important to you doesn't mean that she 'can't do anything right,'" I said. Then I went on to suggest that she think of something the 'can't do anything right' daughter manages to do that does make her happy. After some thought, Brenda answered, "She travels a lot, and whenever she sees a piece of jewelry or a particular book she knows I would like, she always buys it for me." "So," I gently suggested, "she thinks of you during her many travels, and selects just the right something that she thinks you would enjoy, right?" "I guess so," Brenda answered, "but I never thought of it that way." She was pleased to see that each of her three kids had a different way of showing their appreciation.

> ***TAKE AWAY:*** *An understanding parent knows that you simply can't get everything you want from one child. That's why it's smart to enjoy what each of them gives you.*

Lois found her herself in a similar situation after hearing upsetting news during an annual breast exam.

Lois' Story

Three years ago, when Lois was diagnosed with breast cancer, both her girls were by her side, not only during surgery, but also with their support during her awful chemotherapy and radiation treatments.

Fast forward to post-recovery days when her older daughter calls every day just to check in, but Lois hardly ever hears from the younger child. Not intentionally hoping to instill guilt in order to get her daughter to call more often, Lois took the "in your face" approach, and during their next cell phone conversation made sure to let her somewhat-aloof daughter know that her sister calls EVERY SINGLE DAY.

Lois' comment boomeranged because the younger sister shot back defensively "I was there during surgery and chemo, when it really mattered – wasn't I? Not everyone can be as PERFECT as my sister!" she said, and slammed down the phone.

> **TAKE AWAY:** *You don't have to be a genius to realize that Lois made her daughter feel as if she wasn't good enough, and that her efforts just didn't measure up to her sister's.*

My Story

I learned a BIG lesson about not talking to one sibling about another (or even about their spouses or children) when I shared with Laurie, my oldest daughter, an issue that one of her sisters was having with her husband. When Laurie called, her intention was to give her sibling some advice on marriage. "Who told you that?" her sister asked Laurie. "Well, when I was talking to mom, she suggested that I might be able to help you," answered Laurie. Before Laurie could even say another word, her sister hung up the phone. And you can guess who she called next! "Mom, what I tell you is for your ears only. I can't ever trust you again." Bang went the phone. I called back to apologize, and since that day I have never shared anything that one daughter has told me about another. And for that matter, I learned not to discuss their issues with anyone – unless I ask permission to do so first.

> ***TAKE AWAY:*** *Keep each family member's information and confidences in a private compartment.*

Annette's Story

Annette discovered that she'd unintentionally created conflict when her younger daughter, Vicky, gave her the cold shoulder – which was Vicky's standard way of expressing jealousy. Why? Annette's other daughter, Marian, has twin sons who are high school seniors, and their goal is to attend Harvard, but Vicky's son, who is also a high school senior, will be lucky to get admitted into a local community college. Proud about the Harvard-bound grandkids, Annette constantly updates their achievement to everyone in the family, but rarely – if ever – mentions the other grandson's progress. Vicky is hurt, and she feels like the failed daughter/parent.

In Annette's eyes, if her heirs go to an Ivy League college, friends will regard her as the matriarch of an intelligent, successful family. But grandchildren's lives shouldn't be about grandparents' ego trips.

> **TAKE AWAY:** *Grandparents would come across as a much more loving if they found something special to brag about in each of the grandchildren!*

Competition between siblings can also be created when parents help or support one child more than another. That's the problem the Stevensons, who live in Las Vegas, faced when their daughter, Anne, accused them of financially bailing out her brother, Roland, who could never keep a job and seemed to always live beyond his means.

The Stevensons' Story

Seymour and Shirley Stevenson were proud of Anne, a high-powered attorney who never asked them for anything, but couldn't help feeling sorry for their son. So they were surprised when, at a family gathering, Anne exploded and accused Roland, her brother, of being the squeaky wheel of the family. She turned to her parents and said, "You're always helping him financially, and you run to babysit his kids whenever he whistles. But I can't even remember the last time you offered to help me out!"

Surprised and confused by their daughter's outburst when she called Roland a squeaky wheel, the Stevensons sought advice from their pastor. He explained to them that her angry outburst was an expression of her jealousy. He told them, "Anne sees herself as the quiet, reliable, hardworking wheel, while her brother gets plenty of 'grease' for his lack of work." Then he advised them to tell Anne that they simply hadn't realized how she felt. "Now that you are aware of her resentment," the pastor added, "ask Anne how you might be of help to her. Anne still might not want anything, but she will be glad that you asked."

> **TAKE AWAY:** *Just because your child appears to be self-sufficient, don't assume that he or she no longer needs you.*

Problems between siblings can – understandably – be aggravated when a son-in-law or daughter-in-law enters the picture. They say *you can't choose your family*, but if you take that promise one step further, *you also can't select who your children bring into the family.* This too, can create sibling rivalry. For example, a sister may feel that her new sister-in-law took away her close childhood confidant, or that a brother is jealous of the wealthy man his sister married. Phyllis and Bert found that their married children had "sibling-in-law" rivalry, which created tension for them.

Phyllis and Bert's Story

This boomer-age couple is thrilled that both their daughter and son are married with children: they are saddened, however, that they can never get the whole family together for holidays or celebrations.

Their daughter, Roberta, refuses to have anything to do with her brother's wife, Janice. Roberta doesn't even want to be in the same room with her sister-in-law because (evidently) she is jealous that Janice has a drop-dead figure, while she struggles to fit into a size 16. Janice doesn't know why she is always given the cold shoulder, and both women try to avoid family functions if the other sister-in-law will be there.

To avoid friction, Phyllis and Bert wind up making two separate Thanksgiving dinners (one for each of their children and their families) It's exhausting (and expensive) for these grandparents to do double duty in the kitchen.

While Phyllis and Bert can't make friends of enemies, they can share their feelings with each couple. A dialogue could go something like this, suggests Psychotherapist Ann Bair. *"It's so hurtful to us (or Bert and me, or Phyllis and me) that you can't see your way to come together for the holidays. Although I understand that there might be issues between the two of you, I do expect both of you to be respectful enough to care about **our** feelings and put aside your conflict for a few* *hours. It would make us so happy for the entire family to come together – for a few important dates each year – to our holiday table. More important, you would also set a good example for your children."*

> **TAKE AWAY:** *Wise parents know that they can't control their adult children's rivalries, but they can expect their offspring be grown up enough to share holidays together.*

Another common complaint is typical of parents who want their children close, but can't seem to foster their relationship. This is Pearl's issue.

Pearl's Story

"My two sons, who were good friends in childhood, hardly ever speak now that they are adults," said Pearl. "One is married; the other is gay and single. While I'm constantly giving hints that they should call each other, they ignore my wishes," she said. "When I'm gone," I tell them, hoping to give them a little guilt, "you'll only have each other."

All parents want to see their children feel close to each other in childhood and remain so as adults. But the truth of the situation is that there's not much parents can do to keep their children united. There is, however, one thing that definitely goes under the "don't do" list: nagging your grown kids to call each other. That decision must come from *their hearts*, and not be because their mother pesters them. Just because your kids aren't in touch on a regular basis, doesn't mean they won't be there for each other in times of crisis or difficulty.

> *TAKE AWAY: Siblings share an evolving bond that ebbs and flows through the years, whether we're there to witness it or not.*

CHAPTER WRAP-UP

- Respect each child for his or her unique qualities; don't make comparisons.
- Let each sibling decide when and how to share his or her own good (or bad) news; don't be the family messenger.
- Don't "compare" grandchildren; it can be hurtful to them and to your children.
- Just because your child appears to be self-sufficient, don't assume he or she doesn't need you.

- The sibling in-law rivalry is different from sibling competition, but both warrant compassion and understanding.
- Closeness between adult siblings should come from their hearts; not from a pestering parent.

CHAPTER THREE

MONEY MATTERS
To Aid or Not To Aid

"Give a man a fish and you feed him for a day; teach him to fish, and you feed him for a lifetime."

Old Chinese Proverb

As parents, we certainly know about cutting a newborn's umbilical cord, but few of us ever talk about cutting our adult kids money cord. And for good reason. Dealing with finances – theirs, ours, or what our kids think they will someday inherit from us – is one of the most confusing and thorny interactions between parents and their adult children. On the one hand, we want to be there and be supportive for our grown children, but on the other hand, it's time they took care of themselves.

Many of today's senior-age parents – who were of a "savings generation" – have over the years acquired greater wealth then our adult children currently enjoy. These parents were frugal and cautious about money because having lived through (or because they remember – or heard about – their own parents having lived through) the financial crisis of the stock market crash of 1929, and its aftermath. They darned their socks, drove the same car for years, and would never have dreamt of leasing pricey new vehicles every few years.

Our offspring – who are in their 20's, 30's and even 40's – don't have disturbing memories of surviving that long-ago financial downturn (when the national unemployment rate was 25%), so it's difficult to convince our children to *save for a rainy day* when they have never really experienced a rainy day, let along a financial tsunami.

Our children only know the easy path to money because they've had the freedom to live the high life without anxiety. Thanks to easy access to credit cards from companies who got our kids hooked on them as soon as they turned 18, these youngsters have lived with a *buy now, pay later* mentality.

Of course, due to our country's recent financial decline, much of that is changing. And many young people today are surprised to find themselves deep in debt as a result of having spent more money than they should have. So they are turning to their parents to bail them out or to bankroll their extravagant "needs." It's a generational shift, because in the past children used to take care of their elderly parents.

So it's no wonder that today's older generation is in a quandary about whether or not to give money to (or even to help out) their "financially distressed" children. If we have extra cash, do we give it to our kids to make their lives easier – or do we let them figure out their finances for themselves (like we did)?

It's a tough question with very complex answers, especially because those of us who raised our children by giving them whatever they wanted – whenever they wanted it – essentially encouraged the elevated lifestyle to which they became so accustomed.

Giving money to an adult child is a topic that has no right or wrong answers. Ask ten parents for their opinion and you're sure to get ten different answers because each family's situation is different. But after speaking about this topic to experts over the years, I've learned that – when it comes to money – a universal rule can be applied. Remember how the airline flight attendant tells the passengers that "in case of an emergency" the adult passengers should put their life-saving oxygen mask on first, and then assist their children? Well, when it comes to money, the same advice applies – protect yourself first, then help your children.

Our decisions, say the finance mavens, warrant a lot of soul searching because money represents much more than simply its purchasing power. Money, for many parents, can serve as an emotional connection with their children. It's a tangible way for them to keep the apron strings firmly tied, whether it's with a generous down payment for a house or a fancy extended-family vacation.

Outwardly, financial gifts may appear to be a thoughtful way to express generosity, but it's often a way to forestall an aging parent's loneliness when grown children find their own way in life. By tightly holding onto the money cord, parents can have control over the lives of their children, and feel both needed and important. It can also make parents feel powerful, and make their adult children feel subservient and obligated. The dynamic becomes more like a parent and a young child, rather than the healthy interaction of a mature parent and an adult child.

"The line between generosity and control is a fine one," says Dr. Ruth Nemzoff, author of ***Don't Bite Your Tongue: How To Foster Rewarding Relationships With Your Adult Children.*** "When strings are attached to a financial gift, it becomes tangled in a web of obligations, duties and expectations," she said. "Manipulation or bribes (giving money, promising an inheritance, and supporting lifestyles) to keep them connected will only serve to increase distance and resentment."

According to Nemzoff, a healthier way to stay close to your children is through honest communication. In her book she explains that "While exposing one's feelings can be risky, trying to control your adult children also has a price. It can lead to cutting off conversation and connection." Nemzoff writes about Jan, because this scenario serves as a good example of how parents often give their children mixed messages when they say one thing, but really mean something else.

Jan's Story

Jan wanted to move away from her small town outside of New York to study art in the Big Apple. But when she shared this goal with her parents, they said they would only help pay for her education (manipulation and bribe) if she stayed close to home.

Jan felt controlled; she resented that her parents would only help her out if she followed their guidelines, and did it their way. She didn't understand their fear that New York would change Jan, that the big city would make her more worldly, that she might eventually marry a "city slicker" and never return to their small town.

Had Jan understood their fears, an honest discussion might have ensued, and both parties could have understood that it wasn't about the money; it was about her parents' fear of losing the connection they felt with their only child, writes Nemzoff.. The key, then, she explains is for a lonely parent to a) be in touch with his or her feelings, b) be able to communicate those feelings with the children, and c) find healthier ways to stay connected.

> **TAKE AWAY:** *Sometimes financial dissention between parents and adult children has less to do with dollars and cents than with issues of the heart.*

One of my newspaper readers, who said she was consistently giving her grown son money whenever he asked for it out of fear of his anger and/or rejection, wrote to ask me what the difference was between **enabling** your children by giving them money as opposed to **helping** them. Angelyn Miller, author of ***The Enabler: When Helping Hurts the One You Love***, addressed the confusion by explaining "Helping means you're doing something for someone who can't do it for himself. Enabling is doing something for someone who can – and should – do it for himself. The more you give to (enable) your adult children, the more they will depend on you, and less on themselves."

Eva's Story

Eva was a widow who lived on a fixed income. Although she enjoyed simple pleasures like going out to dinner (early-bird specials) and to the movies with friends, she was lonely and missed the closeness she once had with her son, Fred, a 30-year old college graduate who habitually lived beyond his means.

Because Fred was always in debt (he liked fancy cars and trips to Vegas), Eva would invariably bail him out. The more he asked, the more she gave because she feared his anger or rejection if she turned him down. She couldn't say "no" to her baby, she told me, until the day she learned that her bank account had a zero balance. Eva believed that if she encouraged her son to lean on her, he would never leave her.

A family counselor helped Eva understand that by constantly rescuing her son she was really denying him the ability to become monetarily independent and self-reliant. His financial dependency on her – or her habit of enabling him – was not only doing him a disservice, but it was putting her in the poor house, as well.

Eva slowly learned to say "no" to her son, in spite of the old fear of losing her son's love, which had – in the past – led her to cave in to his demands.. Fred gradually became proud of his newfound feeling of economic independence and, with time became financially self-sufficient.

Recently, I spoke with Eva after she had just returned home from having dinner with Fred at a local restaurant. "Guess what," she said "he picked up the check and said 'Mom, this one is on me!'" It took more than a year for Eva to turn things around between them, but she now clearly sees that she could still have a close, loving, and much healthier relationship with her son after cutting the money cord that she felt was needed to keep him tied to her.

> ***TAKE AWAY:*** *When parents serve as a constant life preserver, a child thinks of himself as incapable of making it to shore, so to speak, on his own.*

Lorraine and Sam Benders money issue was different. Their son, Bob, was in dire financial straits, and the Benders wondered whether or not they should – as well as how they could – help him.

The Benders' Story

When Bob, a hard-working married man with two small children learned that he needed expensive dental work to save his teeth, he planned to pay for the procedure by taking out a bank loan that came with a hefty interest rate.

Lorraine and Sam, although not wealthy by a long shot, wanted to help out, but were worried that any money they might give him would put a dent in their modest retirement fund. "Bob has never asked us for a penny," said Sam, "but even though we couldn't pay the entire dental bill, we both wanted to do something to help out."

So, the couple decided on a compromise. They would lend Bob the money (interest – free, with a long period of time to pay it back), and they drew up a simple payment agreement so both parties would fully understand the obligations involved. The Benders were comfortable with their decision because the money was being used for an important reason, rather than for a fancy car or a non-essential luxury. (Lorraine and Sam could have also chosen to pay a portion of the bill directly to the dentist, and thereby gained points on their credit card.)

For these parents, the line between ***enabling*** their son and lending a helping hand when it was really needed was very clear. (Keep in mind, though, that when it comes to money and your adult children, there are no *must do's*; only *want to do's* and simply *can do's*.)

> **TAKE AWAY:** *When bailing out an adult child, a loan with specific terms and a written payback agreement – rather than an outright gift – should be considered.*

Clear communication is important between parents and adult children when money is being offered to help solve a specific problem.

When parents feel unappreciated for the financial assistance offered to an adult child, or when their expectations of how the money should be spent differ from their child's view, resentment can build. The failure to "earmark" where the money will go can cause unpleasant complications for the person writing the check. The following story illustrates what can happen when the giver and the recipient are not on the same page.

John's story

John offered to help his son, Seth, wipe out his substantial credit card debt so that the young man could operate with a clean slate and restructure his finances. John happily put a check for $10,000 in the mail, because he knew how stressful it is for a family man to be in debt. But two months later, when John went to visit Seth, he noticed a brand-new Lexus SUV parked in the driveway, and asked his son how he'd managed to afford a new car when he'd had so many overdue bills.

John had assumed that his check had been used to pay off debts, but Seth had used the money as a down payment for his shiny new car. When the now-confused father asked his son why he had splurged on a new car and put himself even deeper into debt, the son replied "Surely you don't expect me to live in this neighborhood and keep driving my old Honda, do you?"

No one can blame John for being hurt and disappointed by his son's irresponsibility, but he learned a valuable lesson.

> *TAKE AWAY: Both parents and children should be on the same page when it comes to how "gifted" money will be spent.*

Parents don't want their children to view them as the local, no-questions-asked banker or ATM machine, because they'll feel free to return again (and again) for a hassle-free handout.

But what happens when a mature parent is caught between two generations who both need her help? Brenda felt that she was being taken advantage of when her son and his wife asked her to pay for her grandson's college tuition. But things turned out ok in the end.

Brenda's story

Over lunch one day, Brenda told me how she had scrimped and saved to send her kids to college. "I never thought of asking my parents to help me pay for their tuition, she said. "But now, my kids have been living large, and are financially way over their heads. They have a new BMW every year and enjoy fancy vacations in the Bahamas, when they should have been saving for Tim's education. I'm angry that they don't see his tuition as THEIR responsibility, rather than mine. But, on the other hand, I don't want to punish Tim because of my anger toward them."

It was easy for me to understand Brenda's frustration, but when her accountant assured her that she could afford it, Brenda decided to bite the bullet and provide Tim with a special legacy from his grandmother. This might not have been the best solution (the experts say that she should have set up a special tax-free college fund for Tim when he was born) but Brenda felt that – in spite of her son and daughter-in-law's inappropriate spending habits – Tim would remember his grandmother's loving generosity, so she paid for his education.

Tim graduated at the top of his class, and when he gave his graduation speech, he asked Brenda to stand up so everyone in the audience could see who was responsible for helping him " get to this special day." It was more of a thank you than Brenda could have ever imagined!

> ***TAKE AWAY:*** *Unexpected expressions of sincere gratitude can more than compensate for feeling used or taken for granted.*

CHAPTER WRAP-UP

- Take care of yourself first. Heed the advice of the airline flight attendant: "In case of an emergency, put your oxygen mask on first, and then help your child."
- Don't attach strings to money gifts (i.e., "IF" you visit/call more often, take care of me in the future, etc.) It's smart to separate your emotional needs and wants from finances. Being resentful can adversely affect your relationship.
- Distinguish between **helping** and **enabling**. Helping means doing something for someone who can't do for himself; enabling is doing something for someone who can do for himself, but chooses not to.
- Remember that enabling encourages dependency. Encouraging your child to work out his or her own problems promotes independence.
- Only give what you want to give. When it comes to money and adult children, there

are no **have to do's**, only **want to do's** and simply, **can do's**.

- Clear communication between both parties is necessary to avoid conflicting expectations.
- Only lend what you can afford **not** to get back, because there is always the possibility that you won't get it back.

CHAPTER FOUR

GAY BUT NOT HAPPY
Accepting Gay and Lesbian Children

"Why is it that, as a society, we are more comfortable seeing two men holding guns than holding hands?"

Ernest Gaines, award-winning author

On one of the mornings when I was sitting poolside with several of the ladies in my community, my friend Barbara passed around a picture of her grandchild. The adorable three-year-old little girl had curly brown hair, a chubby face, and the biggest brown eyes you could ever imagine. Oh, how we grandparents *oohed* and *aahed* over this little beauty. "Who does she look like?" asked one of the ladies --"her mother or her father, your son?"

My friend was silent for a moment, and seemed to hesitate before giving us an answer. And then, with what seemed like all the confidence she could muster, Barbara blurted out "My son is gay: the baby has two daddies."

This group of seniors – who tried valiantly to process the information – seemed flabbergasted. Most seniors today are not yet comfortable accepting gay or lesbians, at least not when it involves either a member of their own family or even the offspring of a close friend.

Barbara explained that little Lisa has two daddies, her son and his partner. In her words, "My granddaughter came to us thanks to a carefully chosen egg donor and a paid surrogate who were each part of the fertility process. Although both men provided their sperm, we don't know who the biological father is," said Barbara. "I think the baby looks like my son, but his partner's parents probably think she looks like their side of the family!" she said, with a laugh.

The ladies looked puzzled, because Barbara's technical explanation seemed like something out of a science fiction movie. But my very brave friend seized the potentially awkward moment, and used it as an opportunity to educate the ladies and show, she hoped, that her experience could help others to become more understanding and more tolerant, not only toward her son, but for all of our children who follow a different path.

Later, over coffee, Barbara told me that her acceptance of Jack's (her son), sexual orientation didn't happen overnight. "Coming to the peaceful and joyful place where I now find myself," she said, "was a process; it took time."

Barbara's story

"Just before he graduated from college, Jack called to say that he had something important to tell us," she said. Though Barbara didn't remember his exact words, she does recall her confusion when Jack informed his parents that he was gay. "He was a star athlete, a great tennis player and a soccer star. Jack had lots of girlfriends, but now I realize that they were just friends who happened to be girls."

Barbara's first reaction was that she would never become a grandmother. Her husband, Steve, had other concerns. According to him, "I feared for our son's safety, and worried that he wouldn't be accepted into mainstream society."

As word spread among her family and co-workers, Barbara began to hear from others who were usually silent on the issue of homosexuality, who were also struggling to accept their gay or lesbian child. Barbara told me that her situation was far from unique. She explained, "Parents of our senior population still see this as shameful and it takes time for us to adjust. I knew that friends and relatives were gossiping about Jack behind my back, but I needed to find something positive in what – at the time – felt painful and negative for me." By sharing her secret, Barbara found comfort and support through bonding with other parents who were also trying to accept what they couldn't change.

After law school, Jack moved in with his partner (who is an architect), and the two men soon decided, like any heterosexual couple might, that it was time to have a family. According to Barbara, the big question was "who will take care of the baby if the two of you are both working?" Jack and his partner laughed. "We'll hire a nanny, just like any two-parent working household!"

And then along came Lisa. "Suddenly," said Barbara, "it no longer mattered whether there were two daddies, or a mommy and daddy – this was one happy couple with a beautiful little girl who gurgles and giggles and lights up my life!"

> ***TAKE AWAY:*** *The arrival of a grandchild can often wipe away conflicts with straight or gay adult children that might otherwise seem insurmountable.*

My talk with Barbara happened years ago, but her conversation helped me accept the surprising news I received when my granddaughter recently told me that she was a lesbian.

My Story

Several months ago, while walking along the beach, my college-bound granddaughter turned to me and said, "Grandma, I'm gay." "Me too," I answered, mistakenly thinking she was telling me that she was happy.

"No Grandma, I'm gay," she repeated again, emphasizing the second of the two words. For the moment, I felt as if a tidal wave had just come ashore and crashed on my head.

"Grandma, I know this is probably hard for you to take, but I don't want to keep secrets from you – I'm gay, I'm a lesbian."

My head was exploding with questions. "Sweetie, when did you first find out? Are you really sure about this?" My inquiries came pouring out like the oil that had recently begun gushing into the Gulf of Mexico. I was hoping that she would say, "Oh Grandma, I'm only kidding," but the look on her face told me that there was nothing funny about what she had just said. My granddaughter was "coming out" (this is the phrase that's used when someone has chosen to let others know that he or she is gay or lesbian) to me, and I knew that I needed to be supportive – as never before – to such a sensitive piece of news.

Looking at her pretty, sun – kissed face, I told her that as far as I was concerned being a lesbian was perfectly fine in my books. But the truth was, at that moment, I really didn't feel that way.

Theoretically, I've always felt that it's a good thing our society has become more accepting of diversity among people – and that includes gays and lesbians. But on that day, I guess I talked the talk, but was not yet ready to walk the walk. It simply hit too close to home, and at the time I wasn't so sure that I could accept my granddaughter's unexpected news.

Because I knew how difficult it was for her to tell me, I decided to speak from my heart and wound up saying something like, "You are still the love of my life, and whatever makes you happy, makes me happy, too."

This beautiful young woman broke into a big smile, and was obviously relieved that she had told me. "I knew you would still love and accept me no matter what. And I'm glad that you understand that my loving a woman instead of a man, is only a part of who I am."

We changed the subject to talk about other parts of her life, including her anxieties about going away to college, the number of goals she had scored for her soccer team, and the dreaded math courses she was taking to prepare for her SAT exams. As we jabbered away, I soon began to understand that my granddaughter's sexual orientation truly is only a small part of who she is. It's just one facet of a fabulous young woman. The fact that she felt comfortable confiding in her much-older (and slightly outdated) grandmother, is a moment I will always cherish.

No one knows for sure what "causes" one's sexual orientation or gender identity. While many theories abound, the general acceptance now is that sexual orientation is an inherent trait, just like eye and hair color. It's just the way some people are made.

> *TAKE AWAY: Everyone benefits when we take the effort to understand that gender issues need not adversely affect family relationships.*

It may seem odd that someone would wait to "come out" until after they have married, but it does happen. The following story is from Ellen, who learned (months after he married her daughter) that her much-admired son-in-law was gay. Naturally, she was blown away by the news.

Ellen's story

Ellen and her husband were ecstatic when their daughter married a man whom they described as "a lovely guy with a good future." But that was six months before a midnight phone call that set the couple reeling. Their 24-year-old daughter who was crying so hard they could barely hear what she was saying, shouted, "He's gay, he's gay; he wants out of our marriage."

Shocked by the news, the couple couldn't get their thoughts wrapped around what their daughter was talking about, especially since the young newlywed seemed so happy in her new role as a "Mrs."

"Accepting a pending divorce was one thing," said Ellen, who had felt faint after her daughter's phone call. "But how could Sophie not know about all of this before the wedding? How could she not realize that her husband was gay?" Ellen wondered.

According to Carole Benowitz, a chapter coordinator of PFLAG (PARENTS and FRIENDS of LESBIANS and GAYS), it happens more than you know. PFLAG is a nonprofit, national organization to support parents, families and friends of lesbians, gay, bisexuals and those with transgender issues.

"Ellen's son-in-law, like a lot of gay married men," said Benowitz, "was living a lie. Perhaps he got married in order to fit into society or to behave in the way others expected of him. At some point, however – which often can take months or even years – a married gay man has to be true to himself and acknowledge his sexual orientation," said

Benowitz, who reiterated that this is commonly called "coming out."

Benowitz advised Ellen and her family to understand that "it's no one's fault. The young man was always gay. Neither his parents nor his wife caused this, and she could not have changed him. He's the same man, except he's no longer a man burdened with a secret."

By attending PFLAG meetings, Benowitz advised, Ellen could see that she is not alone, learn how others have dealt with the issue, and acquire the skills to be honest with family and friends. "It's a safe place to ask questions that she might not want to ask her daughter." (To learn more about the 30-year-old organization with more than 500 chapters nationwide, go to www.pflag.org.)

The more I read about gay and lesbian issues, the more I realized how prevalent "coming out" is today. According to some reports, one out of every ten people in this country (and around the world) is gay, lesbian, bi-sexual or transgender. Approximately one in four families has a family member who is GLBT, and most have least one

GLBT individual in their extended circle of friends and family. But because many are still uncomfortable with revealing their orientation, it's difficult to grasp this number.

While our society has come a long way, parents will understandably react in their own way when first confronted with the news that their child is gay. It could be helpful to realize that Elisabeth Kubler-Ross's general stages (anger, denial, bargaining, depression and acceptance) describe the overall process that many families experience. The goal, of course, is to finally reach true acceptance. Some parents take only a few months to move through these emotional steps, while others can wrestle with the issue for years. Just knowing these stages (reprinted below) can be helpful when it comes to reaching the ultimate goal of unconditional love for your child.

- **D**enial (this isn't *happening* to me!)
- **A**nger (why is this happening to *me?*)
- **B**argaining (I promise I'll be a better person *if...*)
- **D**epression (I don't *care* anymore)

- **Acceptance** (*I'm ready* for whatever comes)

If you're having difficulty accepting the news that your child is gay, it may be helpful to heed the advice offered by Dr. Douglas Haldeman, a clinical psychologist at the University of Washington in Seattle, who also happens to be an expert in gay and lesbian issues. Here is how he responded to a query about gender – orientation acceptance in one of my columns.

"It's never easy to accept the loss of a dream for our children (grandchildren) whether it's a lesbian issue, a divorce, disappointing career choice, even a marriage outside your faith, he said. But be pleased if your daughter or son feels secure enough to come out to you and for that you should feel proud she or he is living their life honestly. For those parents who feel embarrassed to share the news with others, understand that unexpected or shocking news takes time to process before we are ready to tell others. There is no timetable for when to do that; only you can decide when you're comfortable enough to discuss the matter."

For starters, however, it might be helpful to confide in a few trustworthy and supportive friends. They can help speed the process of acceptance and understanding. The most important thing you can do is to love you child (grandchild) for who she is, not in spite of what she is. As for gossipmongers and negative comments (and there will be plenty of that) you can't control what is said (nor should you care).

> ***TAKE AWAY:*** *All that really matters is that your child (grandchild) knows that while you may need time to understand, your love is as sure as ever.*

CHAPTER WRAP-UP:

- Only share information about your child when you feel comfortable to do so. Not everyone is open to accepting a life that is not a reflection of theirs. Understand that being gay is only a very small part of who your child is.
- Understand how difficult it is for an adult child to "come out of the closet' for fear of rejection. Feel proud that your child respects you enough to share his or her inner most secret.

- Being gay has nothing to do with how you raised your child, or any influences he or she may have had growing up. Although some people still think that being a homosexual is a choice, most agree that it is what a child was born with.
- Give yourself time and patience to accept your child's sexual orientation. He or she needs your love and support desperately. Have compassion for his or her struggle.
- Be happy that your adult child can be free to express his or true self; not live a lie conforming to society's standards.

CHAPTER FIVE

THE BOMERANG KID:
When Big Bird Returns To the Nest

"Human beings are the only creatures on earth that allow their offspring to come back home."

Bill Cosby, comedian

Oh, how I wished – after I graduated from college – that I could have been like Mary Tyler Moore. For years, MTM was my role model – an independent, young woman who had a job and an apartment of her own. But it was an era when young women had to either live at home with their parents or (get married and) live with their husbands. Being an independent Mary Tyler Moore-type female in that era was – for me – little more than just a television show fantasy; it simply wasn't in the cards when it came to my real life.

I moved home after college, and because I hadn't lived at home for years, adjusting to life under my father's roof (my mother had died when I was only six years old), really felt like having my wings truly clipped.

But what were my options? I wasn't about to get engaged; there wasn't even a steady boyfriend on the horizon. And to rent an apartment by myself (or even with a friend) was out of the question for a "nice" girl like me, who would someday (sooner rather than later) hope to get married. When reminiscing about our young lives with women of my generation, we often talk about how we moved out of our parents' homes and went straight from our childhood bedrooms to the bedrooms we would share with our husbands!

Unlike my life a half century earlier – when it was "unacceptable" for young women to live independently – today's college graduates are also moving back home, but they are doing so for very different reasons. Today's "singletons" simply can't afford to go it alone. The recession has made it tough to find a job, even for those who have a college diploma. And many of today's young adults are saddled with exorbitant college loans that they must pay back, which means it will take years before they can be free of debt.

Additionally, today's rents are inflated – so living on one's own can be financially unfeasible for young people. Even if a cheap apartment can be found, most rentals are pretty sleazy compared to the cozy comforts of Mom and Dad's place. Some experts argue that the "expectations" of an immature and rather spoiled generation is the reason today's parents make it acceptable for young adults to return to the comforts of home, rather than live in a "dump." David Anderegg, professor of psychology at Bennington College in Vermont, has noted that "Parents used to let go when their children reached age 18, [but] the combination of today's high rents and an unstable job market, plus delayed marriage and parenting, all conspire to inch upward the age of perceived adulthood."

Although the economy maybe the main reason, today's young adults often return home because they're simply not ready to face the world on their own; they still need the emotional support of the home cocoon. Sociologists have coined a word for these live-at home kids – ***adultescents.***

But what if it's not the adult child's need to return to the roost? A rising chorus of psychologists find that many of today's parents – due to their own needy, insecure reasons – have a difficult time letting go of their kids. According to Roberta Maisel, author of ***All Grown Up: Living Happily Ever After with Your Adult Children***, it might be because they worry that they haven't parented enough, or they fear the kid still needs them, or because they are fearful of being left alone.

Such parents should reexamine their reasons for continuing to shelter their grown offspring, Maisel advises, because these types of cases (more prevalent for divorced moms and those in need of companionship) definitely do not help their children. "Resharing" a home only retards a young person's reluctant growth toward independence.

According to a Pew Research Center 2009 report, 20 million people between the ages of 18 and 34 now live at home with their parents; that's about 30 % of that age group in this country. And the latest figures indicate that more than 89 million so called 'empty-nesters" now find themselves with at least one grown child who lives at home.

According to www.Investopedia.com, kids moving back home – or not moving out – has become a worldwide phenomenon, with millions of young people still happily snuggled in their childhood bedrooms. Pundits in America classify adults who return home as *Boomerang* kids, but they are also referred to as *twixters* or *kidults*. The Italians call them *mammon* or mama's boys; the Japanese refer to them as *parasaito shinguru*, or parasite singles. In England, they call them *KIPPERS*, which is a short for *kids in parents' pockets eroding retirement savings*.

Regardless of either the reasons or the newly-minted names, one thing is for sure – new rules are needed today in order for you and your adult child to live harmoniously under one roof. And if the relationship can be sensibly worked out, having the kids back home can actually be a blessing if both parents and grown kids use the experience to establish a mature, loving and compassionate relationship that they didn't achieve in earlier years.

Setting the time, laying out the ground rules, as well as determining the limits and boundaries for what can – and cannot – be done should be established before an adult child returns to the nest. Neila wishes she had known this before her son, Barry, moved back home after grad school.

Neila's story

In college, Neila's 23-year-old son, Barry, majored in accounting, but after he got his MBA, there didn't seem to be any available positions, so he took a job as a waiter. He figured this would just be a temporary step until he could financially make it on his own, At that point, Barry opted to move back into his boyhood room (the one with the posters of famous baseball players.)

At first, Neila (who had been divorced for three years) was happy to have Barry's company. But she had also grown to enjoy her privacy, and had mixed feelings when she wanted to be free to eat her meals in bed, if she so desired, or walk around the house in a nightgown.

Barry also felt an invasion of his emotional boundaries when he returned home to Norfolk, Virginia, where he grew up. After years of being on his own, the last thing he needed (or wanted) was to have a curfew, which Neila felt was necessary to keep tabs on him. "I was always worried about him getting into a car accident, and couldn't fall asleep until I heard him come home," she told me as I interviewed her for a newspaper story that I was writing about problems with Boomerang kids.

Barry had come home to Mom's house, but had wanted to continue living as if he were on his own. "This is a perfect example of two people having two very different expectations," explained Laurie Feldman, a MSW social worker in Norfolk, Virginia, when we spoke about Boomerang problems. Obviously, confusion and tension soon ran rampant between mother and son. "A family get together to discuss mutual expectations prior to Barry's move back home would have been helpful," she said, further explaining that "it's still his mother's home and she gets to make the rules, and Barry needed to understand his mother's concerns."

With Feldman's input, Barry agreed to let his Mom know if he would be home later than ten o'clock (Neila's usual bedtime), and assure her that he would remember to put the safety latch on the door. "Had some previous rules been discussed and set in place, most of these annoyances could have been avoided," said Feldman, adding that "in some families rules need to be written out and renegotiated at regular or monthly intervals. People tend to forget what they promised to do, especially when they think Mom and Dad will eventually give in and do the chores for them – like they did during their childhood."

> ***TAKE AWAY:** Before an adult child 'returns to the nest', both parties need to agree on basic household **issues** before they turn into **problems**.*

Neila's issue seemed minor compared to the frustration Stan Simon felt when his 24-year-old son, John, returned home to Cincinnati after college.

The Simons' story

John thought nothing of leaving the family car on empty after he'd used it, keeping his stereo blasting at all hours of the night, and having friends over with whom he would smoke pot (just as he'd done nightly in college), while Stan and his wife were trying to get some shut eye in a nearby bedroom.

"He's behaving like a 15-year old," lamented Stan, who considered asking his son to leave, even though he knew that John had no place to go. "It's costing us money that we didn't anticipate in order for him to live here, especially since he expects to have three meals a day, plus plenty of snacks on hand – much of which he shares with his buddies. He says he's waiting to get his dream job, and then he'll move out on his own. But so far John hasn't done much in the way of job hunting."

"Indulging their son with all the creature comforts of home will make it more difficult for him to eventually face the harsh realities of the real world," Ms. Feldman commented when I told her about the Simons issue. "This is not being a loving parent, although it may feel like it is,' said Feldman, "It would help If the Simons' could begin a serious 'move out' game plan, even if John hasn't yet found his so-called "dream job."

"Aim for a reasonable time limit for them to move out, and then feel free to offer a few months rent in order to help them get established in their own place," she said. "In the meantime, make it a black and white rule that smoking in the house – pot or otherwise – is absolutely forbidden. Establish visiting hours for his 'musical' friends, and tell him that using the family car is a privilege, not a requirement.'' Feldman said the Simons should remember that it's *their* car, and they needn't feel guilty if Stan doesn't want to let his son use it.

Feldman then suggested that until John is making enough money to move out on his own, the Simons should expect him to contribute to household chores – such as doing the gardening work, cleaning the house, washing the car, etc. Encourage him to take whatever odd jobs he can find to pay a small amount for rent and such expenses as additional electricity, telephone, special foods, cable tv, etc.

> ***TAKE AWAY:*** *Kids who move back home need to know that living with Mom and Dad means they need to be a contributing (financially or physically) member of the household.*

Experts often disagree on how to handle family issues like the one the Simons were dealing with their son. But the best advice I've heard was from parents who struggled but succeeded in moving their adult children forward toward independence. Here are some of their suggestions:

- **Francine:** *As long as our 25-year-old son was living with us after he returned from college and was looking for his "dream" job, we insisted he make some financial contribution each month until he "found" what he wanted – or we would ask him to leave. He wasn't a happy camper, but when he realized that we would keep our word, he got a job flipping burgers at Wendy's, which was four miles from our home. He wanted to use our car or have us drive him to work, but we refused and he walked there and back each day. This was an added bonus, because he lost the 20 extra pounds that he had gained sitting around the house. He managed to give us $50 a month, and when he finally got a decent – paying job as a decorator (his dream job), he moved out. My husband and I were able to return the money that he had given us, which he used towards his first month's rent.*

- **Sally:** *My 30-year-old son returned home after his girlfriend broke up with him and he moved out of her apartment. He was terribly depressed* *and needed the comforts of home, so I let him stay with us for awhile, but then I insisted that he seek professional help in order for him to get back on his feet. Because he had no health insurance, I paid the fees to the psychologist. It was the best investment I could have made, because he's now married and has a decent-paying job. Oh, PS, my son and daughter-in-law are expecting their first child in three months!*

- **Linda:** *"My trouble began when my second husband refused to let my 35-year-old daughter live with us. At first he had agreed, but when we suspected she was using drugs and always hitting us up for money, he insisted she leave. I was between a rock and a hard place because I didn't have the heart to throw her out, but when my husband told me to make a choice – "she goes, or I go" I called for an appointment with a family relationship therapist. I realized I couldn't toss my daughter out and my husband decided to divorce me. I lost a great man because I couldn't stop enabling my daughter. Now she is in a drug rehabilitation facility and I am getting serious counseling and I am learning that I* *need to make a life for myself and not let her destroy it. It's very painful – but the best thing I can do for her is to let her go."*

TAKE AWAY: *A little tough love can go a long way to shoo adult kids out of the nest.*

CHAPTER WRAP-UP:

- Keep in mind that when grown offspring return to the roost (especially if they've lived elsewhere for a time), some heightened emotional tension can be expected. It might take some time to sort out the different interactions needed to deal with an adult, rather than with a child.
- Have an eventual "move out" game plan for your adult child. Aim for a time limit, and have periodic updates and discussions along the way.
- Be clear that even one extra person in the house can increase monthly expenses such as food, electric and hot water charges. Ask your son or daughter to avoid long showers, and get into the habit of turning off lights when not in the room. Until your child finds a job that pays well enough for him or her to move out, insist that she or he take a part-time job to help out with expenses.
- Establish clear-cut rules as to your sleeping habits, and expect quiet at YOUR bedtime

hour. (This means to turn off or lower the volume of the stereo or TV.)

- Unless everyone eats their meals together, a grown child should be responsible for preparing his or her own meals, and can be expected to clean up the kitchen afterwards. (It's no longer just a mom's job!)
- Clarify specific times when your child's friends may come over, and make sure that these visits don't interfere with your schedule or quiet time.
- If you're still doing your kid's laundry – stop. When there is no more clean underwear in the drawer, he or she will start learning how to use the washing machine.
- Have periodic family discussions regarding how the living-at-home situation is going. Members can express gripes, but feelings should be shared in a calm, business-like manner; mutual respect really helps everyone get along more peacefully. Talking about family and household responsibilities is not easy, but NOT talking can create misunderstandings and serious conflicts.

CHAPTER SIX

THE RABBI, THE PRIEST, AND THOU: Dealing with your child's interfaith marriage

"I have two religions, but mommy and daddy each have one. Mommy has Jesus, Daddy has Jewish."
   Claire, age 4, from the movie, "Mixed Blessings."

When children marry someone of a different faith, we parents often feel it's a rejection of the beliefs and values that we might hold so dear. As a group of friends in our over-55 community sat poolside one afternoon, we chatted about the challenges of our children's interfaith marriages. Dave, a neighbor and good friend, was the first to share his feelings. "My wife and I are Jewish, and when our daughter, Sandy married a Christian, we felt she was going against the values and beliefs that are the core of who we are," he said. Barbara, Dave's wife echoed the feeling: "We felt it was a kick in our gut. Had Sandy not begged us, we weren't even going to attend their wedding."

"I know how you feel," said Steve, whose daughter also married a non-Jew. "The hardest thing for me is to see our grandchildren celebrating Christmas and Easter." Jeanine's son, who was raised as a Protestant, but married a Muslim woman, agreed. Her biggest adjustment, she said, is seeing her grandchildren pray in a mosque, rather than a church.

After much talk about our kids' interfaith marriages, the retired rabbi who was sitting with us that day, gave us some input: "When it comes to our desires and dreams for our children, things don't always work out the way we had hoped. We need to find ways to hold onto our values, and let our kids find their own path to heaven."

"With that said," he continued, "you can still share your heritage, customs and traditional holiday foods with your grandchildren, just as you would if you were Cuban or French or Spanish."

Louise liked that idea and made use of the rabbi's advice when her son married a Buddhist woman from Vietnam.

Louise's Story

Louise, who lives in Philadelphia, sent her new daughter-in-law, who lives in Phoenix, a booklet of all her traditional Jewish recipes: chicken soup and matzoh balls, potato pancakes and noodle kugel. A few weeks later, Louise received an e-mail from the new bride. "Thank you so much for sending me those recipes. I tried them all, and thanks to you we had the most wonderful Yom Kippur ever!" (For non-Jewish readers, the humor here is that Yom Kippur is a solemn day of reflection and atonement, not celebration. It's when Jews around the world fast for 24 hours.) While our group got a big kick out of the story about Louise's daughter-in-law, everyone agreed that the young bride gets an "A" for effort!

> **TAKE AWAY:** *Give credit to family members wherever and whenever you can. Praise doesn't cost a dime, but it pays great dividends.*

Conflicts between families often begin when planning for an interfaith wedding ceremony, and those negative repercussions can linger for many years. It almost happened to Ceila.

Ceila's Story

"My tension headaches began the day my son, Phillip, became engaged to a woman of a different religion," said Ceila, who resides in suburban Minneapolis, but winters in South Florida. "When I realized that there was definitely going to be a wedding, my obsession to have some input for the wedding plans went into overdrive. But it was not easy to express my thoughts or wishes, because the bride and her mother were running the show.

"I fought to have a kosher wedding (which they wouldn't do), but the bride's parents – who were planning and paying for the wedding – did agree to order kosher meals for some of our older, more religious relatives. I also fought to have a rabbi marry the kids; but here again, no dice. That's when my son, bless his heart, stepped up to the plate and said that a rabbi and a minister would perform the job together. I didn't get everything I wanted, but in the end, the kids had a beautiful wedding. They wrote their own vows, and both my daughter-in-law and her family made our family feel welcome.

"It was smooth sailing for a few years until one day, out of the blue, my four-year-old granddaughter, Karina, looked up at me and said, 'You don't like my Mommy because you believe in Chanukah, and she believes in Christmas.' I was floored by what she said," Celia continued, "and I told Karina that I loved her Mommy very much.

"But the truth was that I was still harboring some hurt feelings: some from the wedding day, and some because my son and his wife were raising the children in his wife's religion. Regardless of what I was feeling, I knew I had to find some way to build a better relationship with my daughter-in-law," she said.

After listening to Ceila, our group decided that she needed professional advice, and they asked that I write about her problem in one of my Palm Beach Post columns. Here's the response Celia and my other readers received from well-respected Sarasota psychologist, **Dr. Peter A. Wish.**

> *"It seems the issue has less to do with religion per se, but may go back to when you expressed your initial disapproval for your son's marriage to someone of another faith. Not realizing it, you may have set the tone for your daughter-in-law to feel unwanted, not loved. She may have then pulled back feeling HURT, which you interpret as being COLD. Perhaps, over the years, you've responded likewise.*

It takes hard work to melt down an icy barrier, but your best approach is to speak with your daughter-in-law directly. Invite her to lunch. In a calm voice, explain that you are confused about your granddaughter's recent comment. Repeat what the child said, and then allow your daughter-in-law to respond. Be attentive. Don't interrupt her and do not respond defensively. Although it may be painful to hear, seize the opportunity to learn what she feels. Be patient. Wounded hearts take time to mend."

> ***TAKEAWAY:*** *To really learn – and understand – what someone else is thinking, you have to a) ask them face-to-face, and then b) listen with an open heart.*

The group then focused on the biggest bugaboo of interfaith couples and grandparents – the December Dilemma. It refers to the fact that both Christmas and Chanukah happen in the same month, which causes Jewish-Christian couples to struggle with the emotional tug of family memories. During the rest of the year, a couple's religious and cultural differences might not have to be dealt with – but in December, it's unavoidable.

Ben, a Holocaust survivor, and his wife, Blanche, were having a hard time coming to grips with this dilemma.

Ben's Story

Ben, who is an Orthodox Jew, told us how unpleasant it is for him to go to his son and (his Lutheran) daughter-in-law's house at Christmastime. "I grew up in a very observant Orthodox Jewish home," explained Ben, "and seeing baby Jesus in the crèche is very uncomfortable for me. I don't want to *not* go, but I know that I'm not good company when I go there."

"It's often touchy for Jews to be around Christian artifacts, moreso than it is for Christians to be around Jewish ones," explained Mary Rosenbaum, of the Dovetail Institute, a website resource for intermarriage, interfaith family life, and raising interfaith children. (www.dovetailinstitute.org).

"Many Christians are honestly astonished to learn that Christmas, or seeing Jesus on the cross, doesn't arouse positive feelings in most Jews," she said. Rosenbaum suggested that Ben speak to his son and daughter-in-law about his feelings in a kind, non-judgmental way, and then ask if they would be willing to accommodate some of his sensibilities.

"It doesn't mean they should hide these artifacts," Rosenbaum continued, "But perhaps asking them to temporarily place them in area that's not where everyone will be spending the evening. It's a touchy subject," she continued, "but it's best to enter a dialogue than to hide your feelings under the rug. If a compromise can't be reached, however," Rosenbaum advised, "you and Blanche could decline the Christmas dinner invitation, which doesn't have to be seen as a rejection. Thank them for wanting to include you in their festivities, and then ask when it would be a good time to bring the holiday gifts to the children. Be frank about your discomfort, and ask for their understanding."

> ***TAKE AWAY:*** *When it comes to traditions and beliefs, respect is a two-way street. If you show respect to your children and in-laws, it will be easier for them to do likewise. Compromises can go a long way to appease and accommodate everyone's comfort level.*

"It's easier said than done," Sally argued. "Once my kids got married and we went through all that drama about how to conduct an interfaith wedding, I tried to put my uncomfortable feelings aside. Then came the overlapping of Christmas and Chanukah – and boom – all those conflicted feelings came back. It was hard to watch my daughter and grandchildren work so hard to get ready for the eight days of Chanukah, when I felt they should be focused on getting the house ready for the Christmas holiday." (Sally's daughter is Catholic; her son-in-law is Jewish.)

Some of the group agreed with Sally's feelings; others, like Norman, felt the grandkids should celebrate both Christmas and Chanukah. He and his wife host a yearly Chanukah party for the family, and then attend a get-together at his son's house for Christmas. "The world has changed, and we need to move forward with the different ways we each celebrate holidays. If not, we grandparents will be left out in the cold."

CHAPTER WRAP-UP:

- When adult children marry someone of a different faith, many parents resent their grandchildren being raised in the religion of their new in-law. The good news is that there is much more acceptance and tolerance today for interfaith marriages than in a past.
- Even if your grandchild goes to Holy Communion while your son grew up going to a Muslim school, you can still share your heritage. Lucky grandchildren can still learn about and share **your** traditions and customs, as well as partake in **your** holidays.
- Be willing to learn about (and respect) what the grandchildren are being taught. Just as you want your children and grandchildren to respect your traditions, you need to do the same for them. If you are Jewish, for example, you might not feel comfortable attending Christmas church services. But you can certainly invite everyone to participate in your Chanukah celebration, and share your

holiday rituals (lighting the candles on the menorah , etc.)

- If you're upset that your grandchildren are being raised in a different faith from yours, don't vent in front of the youngsters. Having a loving and close relationship with your grandchildren is more important than any religion (no matter how strong your beliefs).
- A good starting place for interfaith grandparents with young grandchildren is to read a delightful children's picture book, ***Bubbe and Gram: My Two Grandmothers*** with their grandchildren. The book shows how two grandmothers – one Jewish (Bubbe), and the other Christian (Gram) – share their traditions with their mutual grandchild. Written by Joan C. Hawxhurt, the text is simple and provides understandable insights for young children. The delightful illustrations by Jane K. Bynun express the grandmothers true love and caring for their grandchildren.

From the book: "*Sometimes Gram doesn't understand the things I tell her about Bubbe's house. She says that's because she grew up practicing a different religion. But she always tells me that it's good to learn about being Jewish.*" *On the following page, of course, the Jewish grandmother expresses the same feeling.* "*She always tells me that it's good to learn about being Christian.*

"*When I visit Bubbe at Passover, we have a special dinner called a seder. Bubbe says that at Passover we are celebrating freedom. We dip eggs in salt water. We eat flat bread called matzoh. After we eat, I get to search for the hidden afikomen.*

"*When I visit Gram on Easter Sunday, we have a special dinner there, too. Gram says that at Easter we are celebrating springtime and Jesus coming back to be with us in the world. We dip our eggs in colored dyes. We wear our fancy Easter clothes. After we eat, I get to hunt for Easter eggs.*"

CHAPTER SEVEN

MIRROR, MIRROR ON THE WALL, WHO'S THE FAVORITE GRANDMA OF ALL?
Competition between Grandparents

"Who other than a grandmother would pretend she doesn't know who you are on Halloween?"

Erma Bombeck, author and columnist

We've all heard of keeping up with the Joneses – the syndrome of making sure that you have a house as big or a car that's more expensive than what your neighbors have. But for those of us who are "of a certain age," there's another kind of competition called ***granny upmanship,*** and it occurs when one set of grandparents tries to keep up with the "other" set, and they become rivals for the love and attention of the grandchildren.

Few grandparents will admit their jealousies in public, but plenty of them have told me privately that they battle to keep up with the other grandparents. This is especially true when one couple is financially able to pursue their grandkids' affection with gifts, trips, and a free-flowing checkbook.

A classic example of this type of competition is what happened to my friend, Carole.

Carole's Story

Carole's son married a woman who came from a very wealthy family that indulges their mutual grandchildren in ways that Carole and her husband simply cannot. "When the grandkids were little, "she said, "it never bothered me when the 'rich' grandma and grandpa gave our grandson a $300 teddy bear from FAO Schwarz at his two-year-old birthday party. My husband and I brought him a toy truck that we got for free after filling up our car with a tankful of gas at a Hess service station. I'm happy to say that it was the toy that he played with all day," she said, sounding victorious.

"But the grandkids are older now," said Carole, "and they are beginning to notice the difference between the gifts we give them and what they receive from the other grandparents." Carole told me about her recent feelings of jealousy when the other grandparents treated her two grandsons to a holiday trip to Manhattan.

"The boys were so excited to tell me about seeing their first Broadway show (Lion King). They rode in taxi cabs, slept in fancy hotels, and hearing about the fun time they had without us really upset me because I knew that all we could afford would be a tee shirt with a picture of the Lion King on it," she said.

"But why were you upset?" I asked. "Aren't you happy that your grandsons had such a wonderful adventure?" "Of course, but I still feel jealous and I worry that they will grow to love the other grandparents more than me and my husband."

When I shared Carole's dilemma with Boca Raton psychologist, Dr. Holly Katz, she agreed that the grandma or grandpa who treats the kids to a trip to New York or say, Disney World, might be the more popular grandparent for the moment, but not necessarily for the long haul. According to her, "Unconditional love is what makes for intergenerational closeness. It's the time spent sharing your hobbies, stories of your life, games you teach and play with them, as well as books the two of you share. People often forget that fancy toys and trendy gifts can break after a while, and all too often kids can grow bored with them."

> ***TAKE AWAY:*** *Time together and undivided attention supersedes everything else, including money.*

My friend Leon, who had a case of Grandpa upmanship, took the experts' advice. Leon feared that his grandsons' "other" grandparents – who lived around the corner from them in New Jersey, while he lived miles away in Florida – would become the more loved grandparents. So Leon wisely devised a unique way to create and share wonderful, fun memories with his grandsons.

Leon's Story

Leon formed a special Men's Club with, as he calls them, "his little guy pals," complete with a secret code and special passwords. And when they do manage to travel and visit with each other, grandpa and grandsons even have a secret handshake.

Their weekly meetings are called to order via video conferencing (Skype) on Sunday mornings, which is when Leon and the boys address each other by their club membership names. No women are allowed in their club, which distressed three-year-old

Steven, who was worried that grandma (Leon's wife) might feel left out.

> **TAKE AWAY:** *Creating priceless memories with grandchildren doesn't have to cost a red cent. All it takes is time, love, and a little ingenuity.*

I could relate to both Carole's and Leon's desire to not be overshadowed when I found myself worrying that I might be playing second fiddle to my daughter's future in-laws who would eventually be the other set of grandparents.

My Story

Years ago, while sitting in a restaurant with my eldest daughter, Laurie, and her soon-to-be in-laws, I felt an ache in my gut when (for the first time) I heard her call her future husband's parents, "mom and dad."

There had been nothing wrong with the food, but I was suffering from an appetite-suppressing dose of jealousy. It was the same feeling I'd had in junior high when Billy asked Peggy to the dance rather than me. The problem is, I am now a grown woman, not a pre-teen. So why was I feeling so left out?

According to the authors of *Grown-Up Children, Grown-Up Parents,* "The reason is rather simple and quite universal…for many parents, the word loyalty has a flip side; *dis*loyalty." As her father and I watched Laurie's show of attention and affection to her future husband's parents, we couldn't help but feel that it was a display of disloyalty to us.

In their book, the authors suggest that instead of thinking in terms of **divided loyalties**, think in terms of **sharing.** But then again, I'm a person who got a D for "plays well with others" on my kindergarten report card, and to this day it's still hard for me to give up anything that I feel rightfully belongs to me!

When I discussed this issue with my friend, Pat, she told me, "If you're bothered now, just wait until the grandkids come along. You and your son-in-law's parents will fight for who's on top," she said. "But since you're the maternal grandmother, you will have the edge over her husband's parents."

I knew Pat was right because of all the stories I have heard from friends who are the paternal grandparents. They are almost universally tales of hurt and exclusion. One friend went so far as to tell me that she feels she's being treated as if she were "chopped liver!" Author Barbara Graham refers to this as the *Mother of the Father Syndrome.*

In her column titled "Are You The Left-Out Grandmother?" published on the website, www.Grandparents.com, Graham writes that when she is with her daughter-in-law and baby granddaughter, she feels like "a third wheel on a hot date." 'But, she understands that in the early stages of motherhood it is natural for her daughter-in-law to seek refuge in her greatest comfort zone – her own mother.

The Granny Diaries: An Insider's Guide For New Grandmothers was written by Adair Lara, who believes that the paternal grandmother has to fight for her rightful place against the maternal grandmother. It sounds brutal, but there is a bright side. She acknowledges that while the Mother of the Father often gets short shrift, there is one surprising advantage. That is, she explains, "You don't get on the young parents' nerves by giving them a lot of advice, because ***her*** mother is taking care of that!"

> ***TAKE AWAY:*** *Just because you're the Mother of the Father, you don't have to act the way you were advised to behave at your children's wedding, i.e., "wear beige and keep quiet!" Accept the fact that throughout history, the Mother of the Mother has always received top billing.*

But competition can also exist between grandparents who are divorced. Sally struggled with this dilemma.

Sally's Story

Sally and Bob have a son, Steve. They have been divorced for years, and are each married to other people. Bob and his new wife are very wealthy, and they indulge Steve and his family with frequent trips to the Caribbean and fancy gifts like iPods and flat-screen televisions. Sally, due to a terrible divorce settlement, can barely afford to give the grandkids Christmas gifts, and she worried incessantly that the youngsters will grow up to love Bob more than they love her.

Sally's concern was making her ill, but then a friend wisely suggested that she share her baking talents with the grandkids. Once a week after school, her two granddaughters – ages eight and ten – came to her house for a baking lesson, and afterwards have a tea party so they can enjoy the goodies they've made together. Not surprisingly, the girls loved this special project with Sally, and looked forward to their weekly get-togethers. This helped Sally stop worrying about her ex-'s largess.

Her granddaughters made Sally's double-fudge brownies, and entered them into a Girl Scout baking contest. When they won first prize, the ten-year-old put her arms tightly around Sally's waist and said, "Grandma you are the best, my most favorite grandma in the whole, wide world." As Sally told me the story, tears welled up in her eyes, and she confided, "My ex may have all the money in the world, but the girls love me just as much – and, maybe more," she added with a laugh.

> ***TAKE AWAY:*** *Every grandparent has unique talents or skills that can be shared with grandchildren in order to create a special, loving bond. All that's needed is to tap into your reservoir of interests.*

Sometimes, the granny competition is not about possessions, but more about who visits whom on which holidays. While we may struggle with the fear of being left out if our kids spend special celebrations with the other set of grandparents, our kids often struggle with worry that they are being disloyal to us if they do. My daughter Kimberly faced this dilemma early on in her marriage to Larry.

Kimberly's Story

Thanksgiving was always the one holiday each year that her husband's entire family gathered together in Montclair, New Jersey. Larry's mom made the world's best turkey and when she passed away, the family felt that it was imperative to keep the holiday ritual of getting together. Since Kimberly knew it was also our family's best holiday get-together, she felt torn that she was letting us down. The problem was quickly solved when Hannah, our nine-year-old granddaughter (who I am sure is brilliant) suggested we celebrate two Thanksgivings – one day with Papa Joe's family and another day with us. Problem solved.

> **TAKE AWAY:** *Once again, thorny issues can often be solved with a little creative advance planning. Rather than obsess about the family traditions that have changed, consider new ways to celebrate holidays.*

In theory, this all sounds so sensible. But while we may not be proud of our anxious, competitive feelings, it's important to remember that we don't need to act on them. Simply acknowledging them, talking to friends about how we feel (even to a shrink if it gets that bad), can help us avoid behaving like self-centered teenagers who are out to win a popularity contest!

CHAPTER WRAP-UP

- It's not unusual for grandparents to feel jealous of or competitive with the other set of grandparents. Acknowledging those feelings, however, makes it easier to move on.
- Money and expensive gifts are not the most valuable things you can give your grandkids. The unconditional love, time and attention that they get from their grandparents is what they will remember long after you are gone.
- Try to create youthful, childlike games to bond with your grandchildren. Youngsters love grandparents who can play like a kid with them.
- Regardless of how much the Mother of the Father wants to feel just as (if not more) important than the Mother of the Mother when a newborn grandchild comes into the world, it probably won't happen. Most young mothers will instinctively gravitate to their own mothers first and foremost; it's a daughter-in-law's comfort zone, so just be

patient and accept second billing.
- To avoid falling into the jealousy trap, figure out a special talent or interest that you have, and then share that gift with your grandchildren. They will always remember the time you spent bonding together during a shared activity.
- Holidays and family get-togethers can create jealousy when the children and grandkids go to the other relatives' homes more often than they come to visit your side of the family. Solve this thorny problem with advance planning – you know, "this holiday you come to our home, the next one you go to theirs." Annual calendars (paper or digital) come in handy, especially if everyone is on the same page.

CHAPTER EIGHT

WOMEN AT WAR: MAKING FRIENDS WITH YOUR DAUGHTER-IN-LAW
The Underlying Conflicts of Loving The Same Man

"The grumbling mother-in-law forgets that she was once a daughter-in-law."

Greek proverb

We're a society that makes jokes about in-laws, especially about mothers-in-law. Perhaps much of that "pointed humor" stems from the perception that mothers-in-law are the ones who readily express themselves, and often do so without the use of filters. According to sociologist, Dr. Deborah Merrill, author of **Mothers-in-law and Daughters-in-law: Understanding the Relationship and What Makes Them Friends or Foes,** very little research has been done on this unique type of relationship. But, obviously, much of the difficulty between the two women stems from a negative cultural stereotype often seen in books (I Married My Mother-In-Law), movies (Monster-in-law), or on TV sitcoms (Everyone Loves Raymond), where mothers-in-law are viewed as meddlesome, interfering, controlling and cantankerous older women. No wonder a husband's mother is doomed for failure as soon as the young couple walks down the aisle!

Problems can begin early in the marriage when there's confusion as to what the two women can expect from each other. "Think about it," said Merrill, "You are supposed to be loving and happy at the *get go,* but when someone doesn't have the same background as your family, doesn't have your history or traditions, doesn't have your unconditional love, it's tough to treat one another like family."

Differing expectations between generations ("I did so much for my mother-in-law, my daughter-in-law should do the same for me") loss of power and control ("I was the head of the family, now she tries to be the boss") not respecting boundaries ("Why shouldn't I tell her how to raise the children?") and sometimes just plain old jealousy ("She took him away from me") can contribute to the discourse between mothers-in-law and the wives of their offspring.

Years ago, this "Mother-In-Law's Prayer" appeared in Dear Abby's advice column, and even if it sounds a bit over the top, the sentiment is worth its weight in gold:

"O, Lord, help me to be glad when my son (or daughter) picks a mate. If he brings home a girl with two heads, let me love both of them equally. And when my son says, 'Mom, I want to get married,' heaven forbid that I should blurt out, 'How far along is she?'

"And please, Lord, help me to get through the wedding preparations without a squabble with the 'other side.' And drive from my mind the belief that had my child waited a while, he or she could have done better.

"Dear Lord, remind me daily that when I become a grandmother, my children don't want advice on how to raise their children any more than I did when I was raising mine.

"If you will help me to do these things, perhaps my children will find me a joy to be around, and maybe I won't have to write a 'Dear Abby' letter complaining about my children neglecting me. Amen."

But underneath all the jokes, as well as the complaints of losing control or not receiving the attention and/or the love that is desired, the primary source of in-law conflict is anxiety about what we may lose. In her book, **What Do You Want From Me?** British psychologist, Terri Apter writes that the pressing questions for mothers-in-law include: "Will I still be special to my son?" "How much will our relationship change?" and the biggest fear "Will I lose him?"

"Sharing love is not easy," Apter reminds us, and the primitive panic of losing a relationship you treasure can turn an ordinarily good woman into the distasteful stereotype of the big, bad mother-in-law – especially, if like Francine, she desperately tries to hang onto her status as the most important person in her son's life.

Francine's Story

For decades, Francine, the mother of a son and two daughters, was the proud matriarch of her growing family, but felt entitled to have her "boy" reciprocate (in perpetuity) the love and care she had given him growing up, regardless of the fact that he had a busy job, was married, and now had a family of his own.

"When my garage door needed repair, I called Seth and expected him to fix it on his way home from work; I was rather surprised when my daughter-in-law called to say he couldn't come over. She suggested that I hire a handyman! And when the leaves filled up in my yard, I frankly didn't understand why my daughter-in-law was upset when I asked Seth to reschedule the picnic with his family to take care of the leaves. A mother's needs come first, don't they?" she said.

In her book, Dr. Apter explains that this behavior doesn't mean that a mother-in-law is unkind or selfish. It's more likely that she was reluctant to relinquish her status, and is terribly frightened about losing the connection she once had with her son before he got married. To offset that fear, she set up a "test" (perhaps unconsciously) to gain reassurance of her son's continued loyalty. Her method was to routinely request immediate help from her son, regardless of the young couple's own schedules or needs. If Seth answered her every beck and call, Francine figured, it would mean that she was still the number one woman his life.

This strategy, of course, boomeranged. Lisa, the daughter-in-law, was furious that Francine couldn't appreciate her place as Seth's wife, so she began to edge Francine out of the couple's life. Each woman began to press the control button harder and harder, until it was no longer in workable condition.

Things could have been different if both women had been able to understand the other woman's need to control her status in the family hierarchy. With a little insight, Lisa would have recognized Francine's need to remain important in her son's life. And if Francine could have mentally scrolled back to the days when she was a young daughter-in-law, she might have understood Lisa's need to feel like the number one woman in her husband's life.

> ***TAKE AWAY:*** *Some troublesome issues can be eased by taking a walk in the other person's shoes. It almost always helps to look at the problem through the other person's eyes.*

You don't need to be a brain surgeon to know that a good in-law relationship is imperative to maintain good grandparent/grandchild closeness. But too often there is confusion as to what the mother believes is best for her children, and what her mother-in-law thinks should – or should not – be done. Such a conflict went into overdrive for Sally and her daughter-in-law, Dorothy, when Sally brought candy canes for the grandchildren, knowing full well that Dorothy didn't allow the children – ages two and four – to eat candy or other sweets.

Sally's Story

While Sally said she could understand that her daughter-in-law tried to feed her children only healthful foods, she was appalled that the younger woman was so rigid that she wouldn't allow the children to enjoy the once-a-year Christmas treats! "After all, she said, "candy canes and gingerbread cookies were always my son's favorites. Even when he went off to Afghanistan (he had served as a Marine) we'd pack up and sent off pounds of those goodies for him to share with his buddies. So this year before we went to visit with our children and grandchildren for Christmas dinner," said Sally, "I threw in a couple of candy canes and a small box of my homemade gingerbread cookies into my handbag, JUST IN CASE my controlling daughter-in-law, Dorothy, would give in and let the children enjoy their holiday treats (just as their Daddy had done when he was growing up.) I didn't say a word about it when I got to their home, but the aroma of the cookies prompted my little granddaughters to ask what was in my handbag."

Sally continued, "I wasn't going to lie, and told them that they needed to ask their mother if they could have some. The look on Dorothy's face from across the room was evil enough to give me a heart attack! She, of course, had to say 'yes' – and frankly, I felt victorious! She didn't speak to me for the entire evening. To this day, in fact, she won't take any of my phone calls, and when I come to visit she is conveniently out shopping or taking a walk with a friend. Frankly, I think she is taking this holiday treat issue way too seriously; her anger is unjustified, but I don't know how to resolve the situation."

Hearing Sally's complaint, I asked retired psychoanalyst, Ruth Kesslin, whether Sally realized that she had created a major rift in her relationship with her daughter-in-law by overstepping her bounds.

"A grandmother's role is to be a soft place to fall, and not the maker of rules. It's a mom and dad's job to do that," said Kesslin, originally from Manhattan and who now facilitates senior women's self-help groups in Palm Beach Gardens, Florida. When Dorothy said "no candy" – and grandma brought it anyway – Sally set up a triangle between herself, her granddaughters and her daughter-in-law. Three misaligned people in a relationship just doesn't work.

"Also," added Kesslin, "the harsh words 'I felt victorious" jumped out at me, because when someone wins, someone also loses. And in this case, Sally's potential estrangement with her daughter-in-law outweighs any winning situation.

Kesslin suggests that before the rift becomes deeper, a wise Sally would first offer an apology to her daughter-in-law, and then remind herself that her son and his wife are the heads of their own nuclear family – and grandma's place is to follow their lead. When that happens, Sally can feel truly "victorious."

> *TAKE AWAY: When it comes to the grandchildren, make sure to abide by the rules that their parents have set for them – regardless of whether or not you agree. You had your turn to be a parent, now it's your children's turn.*

In generations before us, it was the daughter-in-law's responsibility to care for her husband's mother's needs - even chores like purchasing mom's birthday cards, making the daily phone calls to see how she was, etc. It was all part of her role as family kin keeper.

But today's modern daughters-in-law are out in the working world and are equal partners with their husbands when it comes to raising kids and caring for their home. Many of these young multitaskers say that they have enough on their plates without the pressure of caring for a mother-in-law's needs. This creates disappointment for the older woman if she expects her daughter-in-law to care for her the way she cared for her mother-in-law in an earlier generation. If she feels hurt, angry or devalued, she may act out by being critical of the daughter-in-law. In turn, the working daughter-in-law may then feel unappreciated for what she brings to the family, and further fuels a vicious cycle of attack and counter attack. It happened to Lorraine, a daughter-in-law who was confounded by her mother-in-law's constant complaints about her to her son.

Lorraine's Story

Shortly after Lorraine and Barry married, Barry's mother, Bertha, told Lorraine that she expected her to call her every afternoon around 4 pm, and wanted the couple to come for dinner each and every Friday night. "After all," she told them," that's what I did with and for my mother-in-law every year until she died."

At the time, Lorraine didn't see it as an unusual request. "I was a stay-at-home mom with time on my hands, and Barry was busy building his dental practice." For years the two women got along fine, until Lorraine decided to go back to work as a gym teacher and lacked the time to fulfill Bertha's daily calls and her demands for Friday night dinner visits.

Little by little, Lorraine heard complaints from her husband about how neglected his mother was feeling, and he repeated Bertha's insinuations that

Lorraine didn't care for her anymore. No matter how Lorraine tried to explain that her work load gave her less time to keep in contact, Barry's constant reports of his mother's emotional distress made her wonder whose side he was on – hers or his mother's. Lorraine began to feel more like the outsider than the wife. The couple had numerous arguments that involved Lorraine explaining to Barry that he needed to show his loyalty to her, not to his mother, and he needed to step up to the plate to share her load caring for his mom.

Bertha played the guilt card with Barry ("I'm all alone in the dark, no one cares for me"), which made him confused and bewildered. Finally, Lorraine took the bull by the horns and ultimately stopped calling or visiting Bertha, because she felt that her mother-in-law had created conflict in her marriage with Barry. "I was not going to have this woman control my life," said Lorraine.

Had Bertha understood the generational differences – that today's modern wife is usually in partnership with her husband to care for the family needs (including hers) – she might not have put so much blame on her daughter-in-law for what she perceived (based on her history) that she was being neglected. Barry, on the other hand, could have eased the tension between the two women, if he had helped with some of the things that his wife had previously done for his mom, which would have made it a team effort.

> ***TAKE AWAY:*** *Modern times call for changes in our expectations for family interactions. Responsibilities that were once clearly defined by gender (the wife taking care of her husband's mother) has now become a team effort with both spouses sharing the load.*

CHAPTER WRAP-UP

- Established cultural stereotypes of mothers-in-law (that they are controlling and meddlesome) can negatively affect the daughter-in-law's opinion of her husband's mother. Take the time to assure your son's wife that you are not a stereotype; this will help her to accept you for who you are, rather than what the culture defines.
- Be aware that problems can begin early in the marriage, when there's confusion as to what the two women expect from each other. If misunderstandings occurred earlier, don't dwell on the past. The better choice is to move forward – and remember that love is not an emotion, it's a decision.
- If you feel frustrated about a daughter-in-law issue, take a (mental) walk in her shoes to try and understand her point of view.
- Behind all the jokes is the deep-seated fear that a mother-in-law has of losing the close relationship she has with her son. While

it might take some maturity on her part to understand this fear, an understanding wife will grasp how important it is to be inclusive with her mother-in-law.

- It takes time for a son's mother to relinquish his move from her family to starting his own and to acknowledge she's no longer No. 1 in his life. A smart mother-in-law will be patient with herself (and everyone else involved in the process).
- If you are unhappy because your relationship with your daughter-in-law is not as warm and intimate as yours was with your husband's mom, remember that each relationship is different. It simply doesn't pay to judge present circumstances based on the past.
- Don't expect your daughter-in-law to live according to your standards and values. Things were different in the days when a woman's "job" was to be the family kin keeper; today, both the son and daughter-in-law share that role.

- Understandably, boundaries between a mother-in-law and her daughter-in-law are often fuzzy and unclear. Make sure to clarify what you can – or cannot do – when it comes to the grandchildren.
- Give your son and daughter-in-law room to breathe. Rather than continually making demands for frequent visits to take care of your needs (fix the water tank, take your donations to Goodwill, or check the tires on the car), work on developing your own network of people who can be helpful.
- Acknowledge the natural feelings of loss and separation when your son marries. Allow yourself to temporarily feel sad, and then turn the glass over and focus on good things – like the parental pride you feel at having brought your child to this adult place in his life!
- If you can't let go of your son, rest assured that his wife will make keeping you at a distance her number one priority!

SIX TIPS TO BECOME AN A+ MOTHER-IN-LAW

1. *Don't give her advice unless she asks for it. And when she does, keep your suggestions short and sweet.*
2. *When you come into her home, remember it is HER home. Take off your glasses so you don't see the dust on the furniture or the smudges on the wall. Sit back and be a good guest!*
3. *When it comes to conflict, always remember that the bed is thicker than blood.*
4. *Avoid one upmanship with her. Let her win on all counts. The more she feels you think she's great, she less she will need to prove it to you.*
5. *Keep visits short and sweet, and always call or e-mail before you stop by. No young wife wants to unexpectedly open the door to her mother-in-law if it's a chaotic day or if she's feeling disheveled.*
6. *Don't compare her culinary skills with yours. A wise mother-in-law will ask for her daughter-in-law's recipes!*

CHAPTER NINE

DIVORCE AMERICAN STYLE
Adapting to New Family Dynamics

"There is no such thing as an ex-in law. In-laws are relatives forever."

Tony Fragiacomo

How did you feel when your son or daughter announced his or her impending divorce? Did you go to straight to the medicine cabinet to reach for something you could take to ward off that headache (not to mention the heartache when you learn you are about to become an ex-in-law)? If so, imagine what HRH Queen Elizabeth of England felt when **three** of her **four** children got divorced!

Not only was it a personal family event that became very, very public, but Queen Elizabeth is the titular head and defender of The Church of England. She and her family were expected to set the moral standards for her subjects. And, only a few decades before, she had refused to allow her sister (Princess Margaret) to marry the man she loved,

Group Captain <u>Peter Townsend</u>, because had been divorced.

Queen Elizabeth's children's divorce dramas were played out daily in the media, and gossipy tidbits of their daily lives were exposed throughout the world. There was no bed big enough for Her Majesty to hide under and no medicine cabinet large enough to take away the pain. She had to deal with the embarrassment, the emotional pain, the feelings of guilt and sorrow over the loss of her family's unity the same way each of us must do.

I can relate to Her Royal Highness' anguish. When two of our three married daughters divorced their first husbands, I experienced similar feelings. News of their break-ups (one after 15 years; the other after almost two decades) came with a devastating thud. In one case, we expected the split; in the other, we knew that there had been problems in the marriage, but when they went their separate ways it was like a punch in the gut.

For Ed and me, the news of our daughters' divorces was the end of the idealized family fantasy. The pain was probably no different from the way people feel when there is a death in the family – a pervasive sense of loss, and an overwhelming need to grieve. "This is something that happens to other families," Ed said one night while we were lying in bed talking because sleeping was out of the question. "We've been married for almost half a century," he said, "Weren't we good role models?"

"This has nothing to do with us," I answered, not fully assured that I believed what I had just said. "After all, this is their life, their marriage, their needs. Do we really know what goes on in another person's head or bed? Besides," I added, "This is a new generation where divorce – for whatever reason – is a far more acceptable aspect of life than it was in our day."

Some say it's understandable that when parents divorce the kids will follow in their footsteps, and do likewise. But this is not necessarily so. According to San Francisco psychologist, Dr. Joshua Coleman, author of the best-selling book **When Parents Hurt**, "Even parents in long – term marriages can experience some feelings of culpability if they believe that their parenting skills didn't adequately prepare their child for a long-term relationship, or if they believe that their own marriage served as a poor role model."

With fifty percent of marriages in this country ending in divorce these days, millions of seniors and boomers (unlike parents in earlier generations) are dealing with a child's divorce. "We're younger, we're healthier – we seem to have a stake in our children's marital happiness." says Marsha Temlock, author of **Your Child's Divorce: What to Expect – What You Can Do.**

While it's certainly not an easy journey, many parents of divorcing adult children attempt to help navigate their families through a very trying time, and simultaneously struggle on three fronts:

- helping their children (and perhaps a former son or daughter-in-law)
- protecting their grandchildren, and
- trying to cope with their own feelings of loss, anger and guilt.

Some parents incur heavy financial debt in order to help their children keep a roof over their heads, or they postpone travel plans or simply defer enjoyable leisure activities that come with retirement. Other seniors worry about the loss of a relationship with their grandchildren. For some, it's a challenge to remain friends with an ex-in-law without being (or feeling) disloyal to your child.

For Mimi, the loss of the friendship with her beloved daughter-in-law, Sandy, was more painful than her son's divorce from the young woman. During the five years of Jason and Sandy's marriage, Mimi had spent much time with her daughter-in-law enjoying their common interest of English literature, especially reading and talking about biographies of accomplished women.

Mimi's Story

"When my son Jason told me he had found a new love at his law office, my first reaction was 'what about Sandy?' I thought that he and Sandy had the perfect marriage.

"For months, I would argue with Jason whenever he would rationalize why his marriage had failed. All I wanted to do was to 'fix' things for them, convince my son that he should dump his new girlfriend and to work out his marriage with Sandy. I even offered to pay for the two of them to go to marriage counseling. But the more I tried to convince him, the less often he would call, email, or even talk to me. While Mimi didn't agree with Jason's decision to get a divorce, she knew instinctively that she had to support him. "After all," she thought, "even though I enjoyed a wonderful friendship with Sandy, do I really know what happened behind their closed doors?"

Eventually, Mimi felt that she could do no more. She knew that she had to let go, step back, accept the break-up, and work toward establishing a new relationship with Sandy (who would soon to be her ex-daughter-in-law). What this riddled-with-sadness mother didn't know was how to balance her affection for Sandy while showing support for her son who, by the way, resented any contact Mimi had with Sandy.

A friend who had experienced a similar family issue, suggested that Mimi speak honestly to both Jason and Sandy without placing any judgment on either of them. Mimi told Sandy how much she missed their friendship, and that she would always welcome discussions about their common interest in books. She explained, however, that her first priority was her son, and she could not serve as a sounding board for any complaints against him. (Perhaps when the dust settles – and both parties get on with their own lives – Mimi will be able to resume a more friendly relationship with Sandy.) But for the time being it was clear that boundaries needed to be in place so that Mimi could show support for her son.

> *TAKE AWAY: Whether or not you agree with your adult child's decision, it's imperative to show him or her your loyalty. Staying neutral doesn't always work. When our children's thoughts are clouded with pain – especially in the early stages of a marital meltdown, our child will want proof that you're an ally rather than an adversary.*

Mimi's issue was simpler than those who have grandchildren. Stan and Maxine could think of nothing else but their grandchildren, ages six, nine and twelve when they learned of their son's impending divorce. Their biggest fear was that their daughter-in-law would prevent the children from seeing them, and their concerns were well-grounded.

Stan and Maxine's Story

"When our son, Robert, told us that he was moving out of his home because he and his wife, Lexi, had separated and planned to divorce, we tried to get them back together – at least for the sake of the children. But nothing we said affected their decision. Robert's wife, Lexi, had been unfaithful, and Robert was angry and terribly hurt.

"Lexi saw us as the enemy; she didn't have to be a brain surgeon to know how enraged we were about her role in causing our son so much pain. But the grandkids' wellbeing was at stake, so we knew the importance of maintaining a civil, if not cordial, relationship with her. It wasn't easy," Maxine told me, "to separate our anger toward Lexi, and at the same time let her know we were there for our grandchildren – to visit, to take them to our home for sleepovers, to be included in their birthday celebrations, and to babysit if the children were ill and she needed to get to work.''

While it takes discipline to not bad mouth the in-law who hurt your child, be especially careful not to do so in front of the grandkids. It's human nature to hold grudges, but remember that the "other person" is still the grandkid's mother or dad. If you need to explode – find a friend who is in a similar situation, and go out for lunch together to vent (a couple of glasses of wine can be helpful!). Children deserve the freedom to love both their parents, and we need to model civil behavior, i.e., to be the ones who keep the lid on as rage and jealousy swirl around us.

> *TAKE AWAY: While you may not be able to reconcile your children's marital situation, as Grandpa and Grandma – the matriarch and patriarch of the family – you can help by being a safe port in the storm for the grandkids, rather than taking part in the escalating drama acted out between their parents.*

During the initial break-up, while the adult children battle out their divorce in the courts (which means deciding money and custody issues) their parents often neglect their own needs as well as those of their other children. Pat and Ben found themselves totally immersed in their son Cary's divorce, and the stress eventually contributed to Ben's ill health.

Ben and Pat's Story

"We knew Cary's marriage to Dana was challenging," Ben told me recently. He had a tough time keeping a job; Dana was quickly moving up the marketing firm ladder, and after ten years of marriage she was tired of supporting our son, so she asked for a divorce. Cary fell apart, and we feared he was on the verge of a nervous breakdown. In an effort to help get our son out of his depression, we gave Cary an amount of money (which was a hardship for us) to hold him over until he got a job and was able to get back on his feet. Unfortunately, he never got a job, went through all the money we gave him, and was ultimately still depressed. Naturally, we were now getting depressed along with him. Both of us lost weight and needed sleeping pills to get a decent night's rest. Cary's issue was negatively affecting our own marriage as well as our social life; all we ever talked about was our son's problems. In retrospect, "rather than give Cary money cart blanche, we should have paid for sessions with a psychiatrist to help him get out of his depressive state – something we couldn't help him with."

Experts tell us that while we can't control what our kids do (or don't do) we still need to be mindful about how our help affects our health – and pocketbook. First and foremost, pay attention to your basic needs: get enough sleep, eat right, and exercise on a regular basis. Taking care of yourself will provide you with the much-needed stamina to help your child get through this crisis – and hopefully begin to rebuild his or her life.

Think of yourself first when it comes to assisting your child financially. It's easy to get caught up in the moment of caring, but it's also easy to find yourself sliding quickly into debt at a time when you need to save for your own future needs.

In her excellent guide, **Your Child's Divorce: What to Expect – What You Can Do,** Connecticut author Marsha Temlock gives some useful suggestions to help keep your head above water when your kids call constantly for their much-needed reassurance and support, which she says is very common in the early stages of the divorce proceedings.

"If you're getting calls four or five times a day (including late night calls), there is no shame in setting some limits. For starters, Temlock suggests a dialogue that goes something like this: "Dad (Mom) and I have decided that you should call us in the morning when we're fresh," or "We're really too exhausted after nine pm to take your calls." If you are going out for the evening (which by the way, is imperative if you want to maintain a semblance of a social life) let your children know that you are turning off your cell phone (at the movies, during a concert, etc.) But let them know that they can call you in the morning if they need to talk.

"When you are too emotionally involved in your child's divorce you may become more of a hindrance than a help," Temlock said in an interview for one of my newspaper columns. "Your children will feel the need to not only hold themselves up, but to be supportive of your pain, as well. If you find yourself resentful of the intrusion into what you thought was your new- found freedom once your children married, step back and think of how you are willing (or not willing) to help- and be honest about it. You don't want to add a guilt trip onto your already emotionally-burdened child."

> **TAKE AWAY**: *Keep tabs on your emotional and financial health. It's ok to be supportive, but not at the risk of ignoring your own needs.*

But what happens when your divorced child finds a new love who (perhaps) is also divorced with his or her own offspring? Fractured emotions and fault-finding are already angled with issues such as property settlement, child custody and visitation rights. Throw in the new partner's former family problems, and you've got a perfect storm. The situation gets even more convoluted when you take on a new title – that of becoming a step-grandparent to the children of your child's new partner. And there's more. You almost need a road map to know your place when the step-grandkids have both paternal and maternal grandparents. It's like asking "Who's on first?"

A question in one of my newspaper columns addressed this issue:

Q: *I am a first-time "instant" grandmother. My divorced son married a woman with two young daughters from her previous marriage. The little girls already have two* *very involved grandmothers. One is their mother's mother: the other is their biological father's mother. This all gets so confusing to me! The good news, however, is that I am thrilled to tell people that I have two grandchildren (even though they are not my biological grandkids).*

But here's my problem: I worry that I will be stepping on the other grandmothers' toes when I think about getting involved with the children. How do I partake in their lives without feeling like an intruder?

A: *Many "instant" grandparents ask this type of question. While there is plenty of information available about step-parenting and how to blend two families into one, little is written about adapting to the new role as a step-grandparent. But there should be! One statistic shows that more than thirty percent of people over the age of 65 are step-grandparents.*

The key to developing any new family relationship is to go slow. In your case, the yellow caution light should be blinking full tilt. Not only should you slowly establish a loving relationship with the children, but you are correct to be sensitive to the biological grandmas, who, at first, might not welcome you so readily into the family fold. Coming into your new status should be a process, not an instant event.

For starters, accept your role as a bit player – rather than a shining star – in the children's lives. For example, check out what the other grandmothers are giving the children, say, for a birthday present, and give something of equal value.

The same advice goes for first checking about a movie or special event you'd like to attend with them. Ask to be included in attending the children's special programs – sporting events, ballet recitals, etc. Hopefully in time you will be accepted simply as "grandma," and everyone will agree that three is better than two!

When our children are going through a divorce, it's not uncommon that thoughts of revenge toward your child's former mate may be uppermost in your mind. But these negative emotions neither matter nor help. But here again, grandparents can lessen the trauma by serving as role models for how to behave with civility. Rhoda and Frank learned that lesson after many mishaps.

Rhoda and Frank's Story

"We couldn't let go of the anger we felt over our son's divorce from his former wife, and this negativity often spewed over onto the grandchildren, as well as other members of the family. I remember how I couldn't contain my hostile feelings when we attended our granddaughter's kindergarten graduation, which should have been a joyous occasion. But when I saw my ex daughter-in-law and her parents enter the room, I was filled with rage – especially since she was there with her new boyfriend!"

It's important to remember that anger is a wasted emotion. A wise person once wrote that being angry is like swallowing poison, and expecting the other person to die. In other words, it damages you more than the object of your anger. Years ago, Don Johnson, a well-known television actor, was asked how he handled his anger over the fact that his wife (movie star Melaine Griffin) had left him to marry the famous Spanish actor, Antonio Bandaras, and had taken the couple's children with her. Johnson replied that he loved his children very much, and knew that the best thing he could do for them was to avoid conflict with their mother, because her happiness and emotional stability would only be positive for them.

TAKE AWAY: *In order to arrive at such a mature and accepting state of mind, professional help (as well as the love and support of your friends and family) will be needed. Whatever it takes to eliminate counter-productive hostility and hurt from your life is well worth the effort and hard work.*

CHAPTER WRAP-UP:

- With 50 percent of marriages ending in divorce these days, millions of parents (unlike those in earlier years) are dealing with their child's divorce.
- Accept that a child's divorce also affects the parents. Recognize the need to grieve for the painful feelings of loss.
- Don't blame yourself for your child's divorce. Feeling guilty is a waste of energy. No matter what you think, you really don't know what goes on in your child's bed – or head.
- Work toward a cordial relationship with your child's ex spouse, but remain loyal to your child.
- Regardless of your negative feelings toward your child's former spouse, keep the needs of the grandchildren uppermost in your mind.
- Take care of your emotional and financial needs first – and foremost. It's easy to buckle under the pressure of caring for your hurt child.

- If you are new to the role of a step-grandparent, don't expect instant love between you and the step-grandchildren. Give love time to grow.
- Anger and revenge are a waste of your time. Aim for a place to find peace and acceptance with the divorce of your children, and the ensuing changes in all of your lives.

CHAPTER TEN

MY MOTHER, MY SELF
Seeing Your Daughter as She Wants To Be Seen

"By the time a woman thinks her mother is smart, she has a daughter who thinks she is stupid."

Unknown

Have you ever had a conversation with your grown daughter during which you merely **suggested** that she might want to lose a few pounds, only to have her abruptly end the phone call? Did you ever advise your daughter to put on a little makeup, and have her pop off an unkind reply? The more conversations I have with mothers of adult daughters, the more I realize how difficult it is to understand why even the simplest "chat" can create an emotional explosion.

My neighbor Francine told me how, while she was having what seemed like a pleasant conversation with her daughter, Brenda, she suggested that her daughter take a raincoat to work because the weatherman had predicted rain that day. Almost immediately, the daughter ended their conversation by saying "gotta go" and hung up the phone. Francine was bewildered. "I don't have a clue what I said that angered her so."

I raised this mother's issue with communications expert, Dr. Deborah Tannen, author of the best-selling book, *You're Wearing THAT? Understanding Mothers and Daughters in Conversation.* She explained that it would have been less confusing if Francine had realized it wasn't the caring advice she gave (Take a raincoat) that sent her into a tailspin, but the criticism the daughter heard (she still thinks I'm a stupid 5-year-old.) "By implication," said Dr. Tannen, "a suggestion is heard as a criticism. It implies that if you are telling your daughter to do something differently, then she must be doing something wrong."

Also, past conversations we had with our daughters can affect how they hear the present ones because it triggers memories of the power we exerted over them as they were growing up. If the daughter is working hard to be seen as a capable adult, no longer the little girl in need of a "mommy", then mom's simple and caring suggestion, even something as seemingly innocuous as 'taking a raincoat' could serve as an irritant to her, rather than a caress.

"Conflict between mothers and daughters always spring from an innocent source – the love of a mother for her daughter. But because we care so much, our *curiosity* and *anxiety* often can override our common sense and prudent boundaries," writes Dr. Charney Herst, author of **For Mothers of Difficult Daughters.**

Because these boundaries are invisible, we often don't realize we're overstepping them – until there's a defensive reaction from the daughter, maybe not with words, but perhaps with that harsh tone of voice that goes right to your heart. (MOTHERRRRRR! I KNOW WHAT I AM DOING!!!!)

Learning how to recognize invisible boundaries can go a long way toward fostering a happy, close relationship with adult daughters.

Lenore was confused about the boundaries her daughter, Karen, had drawn in the sand.

Lenore's Story

"My daughter, Karen, works full time and has two young children. I live nearby and would love to clean up her messy home. I don't know how she can leave for work in the morning with dirty dishes in the sink, unmade beds and laundry that needs to be folded. I feel rejected when I offer to help and she turns me down. You'd think she'd welcome my help. In my day, no self-respecting woman would leave the house in the morning unless the beds were made and the house was tidy enough for company to drop in at a moment's notice. But then again, I didn't work outside the home, so I had the time and the inclination to be the best homemaker on the block, if not the entire neighborhood!"

Part of this conflict is a generational thing, explains Dr. Deborah Carr, the author of ***Making Up With Mom: Why Mothers and Daughters Disagree About Kids, Careers and What To Do About It***. "A generation ago there was a lot of emphasis on appearances – especially the way your house looked. This difference between mothers and daughters is often a source of tension; it's that way with me and my mom," said Dr Carr. "I think if I would have to focus on having an immaculate house on top of everything else I would go off the deep end. A lot of today's working women put housework on the back burner and their mothers aren't too happy about that."

In a recent conversation with my daughter, Kimberly, she explained to me that "a daughter's defenses go up when she doesn't feel that she's good enough, or that she doesn't measure up to her mom's white-glove standards. And more than anything else, most daughters I know are always seeking their mother's approval."

My friend, Nancy, heartily agreed, Her daughter, Sally, always got nervous when she, Nancy, came to visit. Luckily, Sally's therapist gave her a workable game plan to deal with her anxiety. The therapist told Sally to greet her mom at the front door by saying "Come in and be a guest in my house – and remember guests don't care if there is dust on the shelves or kids' fingerprints on the walls!" Sally made it clear that this was her house, her turf, and Nancy needed to respect the boundaries she had established. It took time, but my friend soon learned where the line began and ended – and frankly, she said, "I am more relaxed when I visit Sally because we focus on what's really important – not the dust balls floating around on the floor -- but each other!"

> ***TAKE AWAY:*** *The world is a different place than it was a generation ago. It's inappropriate to judge your adult daughter by the housekeeping standards that were important to you. Be a guest in her home, the way you would if you were visiting a friend.*

One of the joys of the mother/daughter relationship is having a close bond with your daughter – a gal pal for shopping, someone with whom to talk about clothing, hair styles, and where to get the best manicure and pedicure. But if a daughter has different ideas, some moms like Patricia, find it difficult to accept that lack of connection.

Patricia's Story

"I was overjoyed when we adopted Alexis. I would have a miniature version of myself to shower with dresses and pretty accessories, and dainty shoes. But as Alexis grew I could see she didn't have any interest in the caring and grooming for herself that I hold so dear. Her feet were large and she was clumsy. She has a love for horses and mountain climbing and had always preferred a pair of jeans over a dress. Recently, when Alexis flew to visit me in Florida, she stepped out of the plane wearing grungy camouflage pants and a hat that matched. I was mortified. If any of my friends saw her dressed that way, what would they have thought of *me*? I used to feel that, as a mother, I had failed Alexis. But, in reality, while speaking to friends who had similar issues with their daughters, I began to understand that it was my fantasy about my daughter not being a mini-me that had hurt my ego. I had wanted to see myself reflected (and therefore validated) in my daughter. It took time for me to stop trying to fit Alexis into the mold of my dream, and begin to pay attention to her uniqueness, her sense of style, and wonderful qualities – which are many. The more Alexis and I talk (perhaps I should say *the more I listen*) the more I learn about her. And although we still don't share my interest in the latest hair styles or what's the best nail polish color, we are learning to accept each other for who we are. Recently we had a great afternoon together – Alexis and I went on a long hike around the lake!

> **TAKE AWAY:** *We can't expect our daughters to mirror who we are. Separate the reality from the fantasy, and accept them for who they are; you just may discover a fabulous human being.*

What we think is best for our daughters may not always be what they want for themselves. Often it's really the dream we had for ourselves that we transfer onto them. This happened to Gina.

Gina's Story

"I was so happy when my daughter, Lois, was dating a young doctor named Fred. He is a rising star at a prestigious hospital, and I felt he was a great catch. In fact, I was already dreaming of the glorious wedding I would make for them. When she broke up with him because she favored Tim, a struggling young painter, I was heartbroken. I tried to tell Lois how much better her life would be with a good provider, but my advice fell on deaf ears. I had always listened to my mother's advice, and I simply couldn't understand why Lois didn't pay attention to what I had to say."

Because Lois could feel her mother's disappointment, she distanced herself by not returning her mom's phone calls, and she avoided any talk of her future plans with Tim. Lois repeatedly told Gina, "Please don't impose your fantasy on my reality." Understandably, Gina was devastated and the two women did not speak for months.

Luckily, Gina picked up a copy of Jane Isay's book, ***Walking on Eggshells: Navigating the Delicate Relationship Between Adult Children and Their Parents,*** and learned how things can boomerang when mothers impose their dreams onto their daughters. In her book, Isay writes: "My parents were determined that I marry a doctor. It was their dream; they thought they knew what was best for me. Well, I obeyed, and guess what? He turned out to be gay!" Gina soon realized that Lois was entitled to choose her own mate – right or wrong – and she needed to have confidence in her adult daughter's decision.

> ***TAKE AWAY:*** *When we let go of our egos, we can begin to realize that it should not be about what makes us feel successful as parents; it's about respecting what our grown children want for their own lives.*

Relationships between mothers and daughters – like all relationships – ebb and flow over the years. Some days we feel close to our daughters ("I love going out to lunch with you, Mom"); other times we feel their rejection ("I don't have time for you, Mom.") When our daughters were young, we were all powerful, and even when they became teenagers and pulled away from us ("You don't understand me") we still always knew that they would come home for dinner. But when they became adults, they also became the ones in power and assumed control of how close or how distant they wanted to be with me and their father. From experience with my three adult daughters, I have learned that it's often best to let them take the lead, deciding when, where, and how they want to interact with us. How close, or how distant we are is up to them.

Another of the hurts I hear about from mothers of adult daughters is when children are secretive about something unpleasant that is going on in their lives. This was really distressing to Julia, when Jake (her son-in-law) was picked up on his third DUI charge, and sent to a six-month stint at an alcohol and drug rehabilitation facility.

Julia's Story

"I thought I was close to my daughter, Hillary. We'd speak on the telephone at least three times a week, and whenever I'd ask about the children and/or Jake (her husband of ten years), she'd always answer with a positive reply. So I was shocked to learn from Hillary's brother, my son, that Jake was getting help at a rehab facility in California to sober up from his alcohol addiction.

"My son asked me to not tell Hillary that he'd spilled the beans about Jake because she didn't want me to be upset. I had sleepless nights, but I kept the promise and didn't say anything to Hillary. In the meantime, she repeatedly kept telling me that "Everything is just fine."

Weeks passed, and when Julia couldn't contain her anxiety any longer, she confessed to Hillary that she knew about Jake's problem, and then she questioned Hillary about why she'd kept his alcoholism a secret.

Hillary's response made Julia realize that until her daughter was ready to tell her, it simply wasn't her business to know. "Mom," said Hillary, through her tears, "I have enough on my plate without having to be concerned about your reaction and your worrisome feelings. Your approval really means a lot to me, and because I wasn't sure that I would get it, I just couldn't risk telling you until I felt stronger."

> ***TAKE AWAY:*** *Even though your daughter's pain becomes your pain, resist badgering her with questions. Instead, step back, let your daughter know you have confidence in her and make sure that you are always available to lend her an ear to listen – as well as a shoulder to cry on.*

Sometimes, a mother really does know best – especially when it comes to matters of her daughter's health and safety. Recently I heard a story about a mother whose intuition and perseverance had a dramatic – and positive – affect on her daughter's well-being.

Susan's Story

"My 42-year old daughter, Cindy, found a lump in her breast, but her doctor said it was nothing to worry about. I knew, however, that for women in her age group, a false diagnosis could be fatal. Even though I've always tried to not be a nagging mother, this time I was relentless about pushing her to get second opinion. Thank God I did, because she did have cancer, which would otherwise have been discovered too late."

> ***TAKE AWAY:*** *Even though nagging can be offensive, when it comes to a child's health and/or safety it can pay big dividends.*

I often hear about how a mother's loving suggestion or good advice frequently falls on deaf ears. But if it comes from a girlfriend or colleague – it is welcomed and accepted. One of the women in my Pilates class, Sydell, complained to me about her daughter's lack of appreciation when it came to her motherly advice.

Sydell's Story

"When my daughter, Celeste, decided that she wanted to go into business and sell her home-baked cookies on line, I was most supportive. Having been a bookkeeper all my working years, I offered to set up a financial and marketing plan for her. Celeste is a trained pastry chef and a wonderful baker, but she knows zilch about making money.

"She declined my offer to help her, and took offense that I had even questioned her ability to start her own business. Celeste assured me that she knew what she was doing, but I was worried that she would lose whatever savings she had. It took time, but I soon realized that worrying is like a rocking chair – it gives you something to do, but it doesn't get you anywhere."

A few weeks later, Celeste called Sydell and told her how helpful a friend had been by offering to set up a formal financial plan for the cookie business. Her friend explained how banks lend money, and even showed Celeste how to keep track of her profits, as well as how to market the baked goods. Celeste's colleague had given her the EXACT same input that Sydell had, but the young cookie maker had rejected the advice when it had come from her mother.

In Sydell's words, "I could expect this kind of response from a sixteen-year-old ("Mother, I can do this myself"), but why hear this from my 35-year-old daughter? I was really perplexed."

When I posed this question to my daughter, Jennifer, she told me that she could understand why Celeste rejected her mother's help. "Although her mother says she is most supportive, she doesn't sound like she trusts her daughter to handle the responsibility that comes with running a business – and that came through loud and clear. Personally, if I were Celeste, I, too, would probably go elsewhere to get the business information I need to embark on a new endeavor. But what I would want from my Mom would be for her to tell me that she is proud of me, and offer to be of help IF I ASKED for it."

> ***TAKE AWAY:*** *Regardless of a daughters' age – whether she is nine or 90 – she seeks her mother's approval. It should be comforting for worrying moms to know that while data and information can come from many sources – it's her encouragement, support and trust that can help facilitate her daughter's success.*

Dr. Deborah Tannen Advises

Are you clueless when your daughter gets annoyed at something you said? Do you feel the need to walk on eggshells when the two of you are having a conversation, fearful that something you say might anger her?

Here's a hint to make things better. Just by changing the way you speak to her (being sensitive, putting yourself in her shoes, tone of voice, etc) can go a long way to change how your daughter will react to you. The following are examples of how "we say one thing, but our daughters hear something else," with tips from communications expert, Dr. Deborah Tannen.

Mother Says: *I called you three days ago. You were taking a shower and you said you would call me back. Boy, what a water bill you must have!*

Daughter Hears: *She is so needy; I wish she could understand that I have enough on my plate without fulfilling her needs.*

Dr. Tannen Explains: *In this scenario the mother thinks she veiled her frustration with humor, but it came through loud and clear because the daughter knows her mother wishes she would call more often. Instead of letting the frustration build, the mother should call* *back and say lightly "You probably forgot to call back; here's why I called..."*

Mother Says: *Hi sweetie. You cut your hair. It's different.*

Daughter Hears: *She hates it.*

Dr. Tannen Explains: *It's a universal fact that any time you mention an aspect of your daughter's appearance – especially her hair, her weight, and her style of clothing – the daughter hears it as disapproval unless it's a compliment. If you don't feel you can give praise, say nothing about her appearance.*

Mother Says: *My friend Sandra's daughter had a fabulous dinner party last night and she works full time, too.*

Daughter Hears: *She thinks I am not as competent as Sandra.*

Dr. Tannen Explains: *Comparison with other people is always risky. The underlying implication is heard as not measuring up.*

Mother Says: *Let me help you organize the baby's room.*

Daughter Hears: *She doesn't think I am capable of taking care of my own baby.*

> ***Dr. Tannen Explains:*** *Any offer to help is double sided. For the daughter, it has an underlying implication that she's lacking or else she wouldn't need help. If a friend offered the same, she's jump at the chance.*

CHAPTER WRAP-UP:

- Past conversations we've had with our daughters can trigger memories of when they were the "little girl" and we were the all-powerful "mommy."
- Learn to respect your daughter for who she is, not for who you want her to be.
- Learn how to be a guest in your daughter's house, and overlook her housekeeping skills if they differ from yours. Behave as you would if you were visiting a friend's home.
- Don't expect your daughter to be a carbon copy of you. Appreciate what she has to offer.
- Don't impose your fantasies on your daughter's realities.
- Let your daughter take the lead as to when, where and how she wants to interact with you.

It doesn't pay to be pushy.

- You don't have to know everything about your daughter's life, nor does she need to know everything about yours. She will confide in you when (and if) she's ready, willing and able.
- Don't offer unsolicited advice. What she really wants from you is encouragement, support and trust.

RECOMMENDED READING

Don't Bite Your Tongue: How To Foster Rewarding Relationships With Your Adult Children, by *Ruth Nemzoff, Ph.D.(Palgrave Macmillan, 2008)*

Dr. Nemzoff, a researcher and resident scholar at Brandeis Women's Studies Research Center, debunks the conventional theory that to keep peace with your adult children "keep your mouth shut and pocketbook open. Because society has changed since you were their age, Nemzoff explains how to listen to what your grown children say and not be so quick to judge their thoughts and views. The trick to having an open dialogue with them is to learn 1) what's important enough to say, and then 2) how and when to say it.

When Parents Hurt: Compassionate Strategies when You and Your Grown Child Don't Along, *by Joshua Coleman, Ph.D. (Collins, 2007)*

Little is more painful than when there is a rift between you and your adult child. And when the estrangement becomes impenetrable, a parent will suffer in silence, not knowing where to turn or whom to turn to for help. Coleman, who is a nationally acclaimed psychologist and author, has written a book that is a great starting point to **help** struggling parents maintain self-esteem through difficult times, **reduce** feelings of anger, guilt and shame, and (most importantly), Coleman offers strategies that attempt to either rebuild the relationship or to move toward acceptance of what can't be changed. Be sure to check out his website www.drjoshuacoleman.com to learn about his teleseminars and small group phone coaching sessions for estranged parents. Also, a discussion board is helpful for parents to share their problems and get input for others who are struggling with similar issues.

When Our Grown Kids Disappoint Us, *by Jane Adams, Ph.D. (New York: Free Press, 2003)*

Adams, a social psychologist, has written a truly helpful guide for parents who are going through a rough time with their adult children. The author offers coping methods for dealing with dependency issues, as well as drug and alcohol problems. She offers practical guidance on how, when and why parents sometimes need to lovingly, but firmly, disconnect from their grown kids and reclaim their own lives – without severing ties.

Walking on Eggshells: Navigating the Delicate Relationship between Adult Children and Parents, *by Jane Isay (Doubleday Flying Press, 2007)*

The author interviews a variety of families nationwide, shares their experiences, and discovers that what appears, on the surface to be an effortlessly good relationship really took plenty of hard work. On giving advice to your grown kids – Isay is adamant: They Don't Want It, They Don't Hear It, and They Resent It. So, Don't Give It. And the closer your advice hits home, she writes, the more your kids will resent it. A former editor, Isay's book is a great read.

The Enabler: When Helping Hurts the One You Love, *by Angelyn Miller (Wheat/mark, 2008)*

Based on her personal journey, the author helps parents understand the difference between "helping" their adult children – and "enabling" them. Helping means that you are doing something for someone who **can't** do it for himself; enabling means that you are something for someone who can

– and should – do for himself, but **doesn't**. When you attempt to "fix" all your adult children' problems, you rob them of the ability to become independent and self-reliant.

The Family Fight: A No Nonsense Guide to Wills and Estates, *by Barry Fish & Lee Kotzer. (Continental Atlantic Publications, Inc. 2003)*

The authors, who are both experts on wills and estate planning, put preserving **family** ahead of preserving **assets** with suggestions for practical steps to take now in order to prevent resentment, even open hostility and irrevocable fights among your children when you are gone. The authors help families deal effectively with the topic of death and finances sooner, when the family is still together, rather than later.

Family Estrangements: How They Begin, How to Mend Them and How to Cope with Them, *by Barbara LeBey (Bantam Books, 2003)*

The author, who is an Atlanta attorney and former judge, shares her personal story of her estrangement from her son, and offers a set of guidelines to help suffering parents mend broken relationships with an adult child.

Choking on the Silver Spoon, by Gary W. Buffone, Ph.D. *(Simplon, 2003)*

Buffone, a psychologist, provides advice to wealthy parents on how to avoid raising children who are indulged and spoiled, as well as how to teach them good money values and work ethics.

For Mothers of Difficult Daughters, by Charney Herst, Ph. D. *(Villard Books, 1999)*

The author, a practicing psychotherapist, helps mothers dispel the myth that if you can be the perfect mother, you will have the perfect daughter and ergo the perfect mother/daughter relationship. She explains how your daughter's unhappiness (neediness or dependency) has less to do with what she believes you did (or didn't do) during her childhood – and more to do with her unwillingness to let go and move on. While most mother/daughter relationship books focus on what daughters can do, Herst speaks to the moms with advice on how to improve painfully strained, faltering, or nonexistent relationships with their grown daughters.

Making Up with Mom: Why Mothers and Daughters Disagree About Kids, Careers, and Casseroles (and What to Do About It)*, by Julie Halpert and Deborah Carr, Ph.D. (St. Martin's Press; 2008)*

Generational differences can create havoc between mothers and their grown daughters. What worked for the stay-at-home mom in her day, will probably not be what works for today's working moms. Both mom and daughter need to understand where the other is coming from if they want to resolve their conflicting issues.

"You're Wearing THAT?" Understanding Mothers and Daughters in Conversation*, by Deborah Tannen, Ph.D. (Random House, 2006)*

This best-selling book by communications expert Deborah Tannen, explains that while both mothers and daughters may speak the same language, they often don't understand each other. Even if a mother's words are meant to be **helpful**, her daughter will often hear it as being **critical.** Because intimacy and closeness – as well as power and distance – are constantly being negotiated between mothers and daughters, conversations between them can open the door for plenty of misunderstanding and perplexity. Tannen breaks down barriers between these confusing differences and helps both mothers and daughters understand where the other is coming from. This insightful book is a "must" for any mother or daughter who wants a more peaceful and pleasurable relationship with one another.

What's a Mother (in-law) To Do? 5 Essential Steps to Building a Loving Relationship with Your Son's New Wife, by Jane Angelich, (Howard Books, 2009)

While most books address the needs of the daughter-in-law and how to get along with her husband's mother, this author offers advice to the mother-in-law on how to establish a good relationship with her son's wife.

Her topics of discussion include 1) to not give unsolicited advice (but be available when asked) 2) to recognize that your daughter-in-law is number one in his life, 3) to give her time to adjust and accept your family (calling you "Mom" may not happen overnight.) This handy guide would make a great gift for anyone who is soon to gain the new title of Mother-in-Law.

Parenting Your Adult Child: How You Can Help Them Achieve Their Full Potential, *by Ross Campbell and Gary Chapman, M.D. (Northfield Publishers, 1999)*

This Christian-focused book provides insight and offers practical tips for relating to one's adult children from 18 to 35 years old. They offer advice on garden variety topics that confound most parents during those years.

Friends for Life, *by Susan Jonas and Marilyn Nissenson, (Morrow and Company, 1997)*

This is a genuinely pleasant read on mother/daughter relationships. The authors share their experiences with their grown daughters and from interviews they had with more than a hundred women across the country. Topics include conflicts over lifestyle choices, communication, and generational differences.

What Do You Want From Me? Learning to Get Along with In-Laws, *by Terri Apter, (Norton Books, 2009)*

A psychologist and noted British author on family dynamics, Apter tackles one of the most confusing of all relationships in her latest book. With extensive research, she pinpoints the sources of tension between in-laws, and explores the way in which we can build healthy relationships as our families expand. Keep this book on your nightstand for easy reference because what's not your problem today with your in-laws could be an issue down the road. To be forewarned is to be forearmed!

How To Raise Your Adult Children Because Big Kids Have Even Bigger Problems, *by Gail Parent and Susan Ende (Hudson Street Press, 2010)*

If you believe that it's better to laugh than to cry, this book is for you. Gail Parent, who worked as an Emmy-award winning writer for TV shows as "Mary Hartman, Mary Hartman" and "The Golden Girls", now takes on serious issues that parents have with their adult children. In a Q and A format with her partner, a psychotherapist, the duo gives sensible answers to often silly questions on the issues that confound us all. (Did your daughter-in-law REALLY steal your son away from you? Do you REALLY expect them to pay back that loan you gave them?) Keep a tissue handy to wipe away the tears of laughter.

Step Wars: Overcoming the Perils and Making Peace in Adult Stepfamilies, *by Dr. Grace Gabe and Jean Lipman-Blumen, Ph.D, (St. Martin's Press, 2004)*

As more and more people remarry later in life, there are additional complications and situational crises that threaten to ruin not only individual relationships, but entire families. This book is the best guide for understanding the new family relationships that emerge when couples with adult children remarry and how to avoid the many painful pitfalls when new alliances form and loyalties shift in the process.

The authors touch on so many confusing issues that face parents in late-life marriages, not only with their own children, but also with their new partner's family. The authors point out that while the new union may be happy, the couple often wonders why their children are not happy for them – some out of abandonment fears or the loss of feeling special in the surviving parent's life, and others due to fear of losing their financial inheritance. This book is well researched by the authors (Grace Gabe is a psychiatrist; Jean Lipman – Blumen is a social psychologist), and should be mandatory reading for anyone with grown children who even *thinks* he or she might take a walk down the aisle.

Your Child's Divorce: What to Expect – What You Can Do, *by Marsha Temlock, (Impact Publishers, 2006)*

It's bad enough when your kids divorce, but what most parents of adult children don't realize that many of the post-divorce issues that come up may take years to resolve. Because Temlock had two sons who divorced, she needed to find information to help her to deal with the new painful issues that she confronted. Her book, which offers a magnum of information, addresses such parental dilemmas as: 1) wanting to lend support, but being uncertain about how much you should do, 2) balancing other family relationships to avoid conflict and sibling rivalry, 3) maintaining communication with ex-in-laws (if there are grandchildren involved) without being disloyal to your own child, 4) being even-handed with grandchildren and step grandchildren, and 5) dealing with the irrational feelings that your parenting was at fault in your child's divorce. Perhaps HRH Queen Elizabeth, the titular head and defender of the Church of England, could have used this guide when she learned that three out of her four children would divorce!

Made in the USA
Lexington, KY
03 February 2013